364.153 VIN
Vine, Cathy, 1958-
Gardens of shame : the
tragedy of Martin
563624

MI June 03
wkDec03

SA AUG 2005
OY SEP 2012

D1736997

Cathy Vine & Paul Challen

Gardens of Shame

The Tragedy of Martin Kruze
and the Sexual Abuse at
Maple Leaf Gardens

GREYSTONE BOOKS
Douglas & McIntyre
PUBLISHING GROUP
VANCOUVER/TORONTO

This book is dedicated to all the people who were inspired by Martin Kruze to believe that their lives are worth fighting for.

Copyright © 2002 by Cathy Vine and Paul Challen
02 03 04 05 06   5 4 3 2 1

All rights reserved. No part of this book may be reproduced, stored in a retrieval system, or transmitted, in any form or by any means, without the prior written permission of the publisher or, in the case of photocopying or other reprographic copying, a licence from CANCOPY (Canadian Licensing Agency), Toronto, Ontario.

Greystone Books
A division of Douglas & McIntyre Ltd.
2323 Quebec Street, Suite 201
Vancouver, British Columbia V5T 4S7

NATIONAL LIBRARY OF CANADA CATALOGUING IN PUBLICATION DATA
Vine, Cathy, 1958–
Gardens of shame

ISBN 1-55054-880-8
1. Kruze, Martin. 2. Sexual abuse victims—Ontario—Toronto. 3. Maple Leaf Gardens Ltd. I. Challen, Paul C. (Paul Clarence), 1967– II. Title.
HV6593.C3V56 2002   364.15'3'09713541   C2001-911610-1

Jacket design by Blakeley Design
Text design by Tanya Lloyd Kyi
Printed and bound in Canada by Friesens

The publisher gratefully acknowledges the assistance of the Canada Council and of the British Columbia Ministry of Tourism, Small Business and Culture. The publisher also acknowledges the financial support of the Government of Canada through the Book Publishing Industry Development Program (BPIDP) for its publishing activities.

CONTENTS

PREFACE

ANYONE WHO KNEW Martin Kruze knew a man who, in the latter part of his life, dedicated himself to raising awareness about the sexual abuse of children. His last year was marked by a tireless campaign to use his own experiences as a child to help others. For many people who knew and worked with him, a world without Kruze's energy and determination was simply unimaginable. But, as his sudden death on October 30, 1997, proved, behind his seemingly unstoppable drive was a great deal of pain.

When Martin Kruze died, Cathy Vine had been working with sexually abused children and their families for more than a decade. She and Kruze had worked together when he volunteered at CASAT (Central Agencies Sexual Abuse Treatment Program), and upon his death, Vine decided that she could no longer continue to respond to the seemingly endless stream of sexually abused children and their families without trying to address the problem in a more substantial way. So she quit her job at CASAT to write about Martin Kruze.

Although the popular media had given Kruze's disclosure of sexual abuse at Maple Leaf Gardens intensive coverage, it seemed as though a great deal of the story remained to be told. As Vine began to meet—and hear about the lives of—other Gardens abuse survivors, she became convinced that these other narratives were central to revealing the whole story. Over the next several years, Vine, and subsequently co-author Paul Challen, compiled these stories from more than 200 hours of taped interviews. Although Vine was able to address the sexual abuse issues that these men spoke about, it was clear to her—and to the survivors—that she knew a lot less about hockey. Challen was able to fill out the sports and hockey context in order to expand the story.

Our goals in writing *Gardens of Shame* were much the same as those of Martin Kruze: to increase awareness and understanding of child sexual abuse among parents, coaches, players, teachers, survivors—and anyone else who cares about young people. But mainly we have tried to paint a picture of the man at the centre of this book and to tell his story in a much fuller way than has been done in the popular media. And because Kruze was such a pivotal figure for many of the Gardens survivors—and for sexual abuse survivors in general—it was important to us to produce some kind of tangible memorial to him, while at the same time including the voices of the other men victimized by employees of Maple Leaf Gardens. We have done this by means of interludes between the chapters, in which these men describe their own experiences. We have relied on their words and those of Martin Kruze to recount their experiences as accurately as possible. In doing so, we describe events that are profoundly disturbing.

In reconstructing Martin Kruze's life, we were helped immensely by several people. No two people, however, recalled the details and timing of every key event in exactly the same way. Jayne Dunsmore, Martin's partner at the time of his death, gave us access to many of his personal documents, as well as many of her recollections of life with him. Kruze's materials contained the names of other victims and references to his family life; if the people named were not interviewed for the book, or if they expressly told us it would violate their privacy, we did not include the information. Gary Kruze also provided us with memories—often very painful—of life with his younger brother, and Martin's father, Imants, supplied many of the missing details that only a father could know about his son. Astrida Kruze always supported the idea of a book about her son, even though she never felt ready to be interviewed about him.

The other people who took tremendous risks in speaking with us are the men who continue to live with the effects of their abuse and who continued to struggle throughout the writing of this book. They believed that the book should be written, and they were our inspiration throughout the long and difficult process of bringing this story to print. Although many of the men quoted in this book have decided to be identified by their real names, some have chosen to use pseudonyms to protect their privacy.

In addition, many kind friends and colleagues helped us along the way. We are especially indebted to two teams of people. First, thanks to our project team of Ramona Alaggia, our clinical research consultant, who offered insightful direction and guidance; Marjory Old, who painstakingly typed our interviews and was inspirational in her support; Don Sedgwick, our agent, who championed this project from the beginning; Rob Sanders, our publisher, who believed that this story should be told; and Nancy Flight, our editor, who compelled us to write it better than we ever thought we could. Second, and most of all, we thank our own home teams: for Cathy—Charlie Keil, Houston and Emma Keil-Vine, and the rest of the Vine, Keil, and Hoad family; and for Paul—Janine, Henry, Eva, and Sam and all of the Belzak and Challen families. Working on this book has taught us to cherish their support and to treasure the joys and teachings of our children.

Martin Kruze, 1962–1997

GOING TO THE POLICE

During these Harold Ballard days, Maple Leaf Gardens
was a sex house for perpetrators and a horror house for
its victims, being minors and young boys.
—Martin Kruze, 1997

ON JANUARY 24, 1997, MARTIN KRUZE placed a neatly typed
eight-page letter, a thick pile of papers, and numerous photographs in a file folder and tucked the folder into a large tan
envelope. The letter, which had been ready for a month, was
addressed to the Metropolitan Toronto Police, Criminal Inves-
tigations Unit. Kruze had driven to the police station several
times before, but he had never made it through the doors. He
had gotten as far as the parking lot behind the building, but he
could not bring himself to get out of the car. Today he would do
it; it would kill him if he didn't.

Kruze got into the passenger seat of the white mini-van, and
his partner, Jayne Dunsmore, took the wheel. They hardly

spoke as they drove to the station. Kruze was worried—yet remarkably calm. After all, he had done everything he could to prepare for this meeting, the most important meeting of his life. He had written and rewritten his letter. Jayne had typed and retyped it. But would the police believe what it said?

When they arrived at the police station, they got out of the car and headed for the building, holding hands as they always did. Today they went through the doors and into the lobby of the building. Kruze told the person at the desk that he was there to report a sexual assault. Detectives Dave Tredrea and Blair Davey invited him and Jayne into their office, and the meeting of Martin Kruze's life began.

Kruze placed the large envelope on the table in front of him and started talking. He told the detectives that he had been sexually abused by two men, Gordon Stuckless and George Hannah, at Maple Leaf Gardens in the 1970s and early 1980s. Then he calmly passed his envelope across the table, and Detective Tredrea opened it and read the letter.

During the "Harold Ballard days" at Maple Leaf Gardens, the letter began, Kruze had been a minor who was "illicitly induced by George Hannah . . . into acts of sexual abuse and sexual assault and in group sex with him and other minors." George Hannah, who held a "senior management" position at the Gardens, laid the groundwork for additional sexual abuse, the letter continued, when he introduced Kruze to Gordon Stuckless, who was employed by Maple Leaf Gardens as "backstage help, dressing room, equipment maintenance, etc." for the Toronto Maple Leafs hockey team, the Toronto Marlboros hockey team, and visiting teams. Hannah was dead, but Stuckless was alive, living, Kruze believed, in Newfoundland. Perhaps he was sexually abusing boys there.

Kruze wrote that he had already telephoned Maple Leaf Gardens sometime around 1992 to report Gordon Stuckless. He was told that the Gardens had been receiving telephone calls and letters about Stuckless and that he was "on trial and being watched by Maple Leaf Gardens." Kruze said it was sickening to think that Stuckless would be allowed to work there at all after Maple Leaf Gardens management became aware of the problem. In bold italics Kruze wrote: "Maple Leaf Gardens Limited allowed a criminal act by letting a perpetrator exist within their midst."

The letter went on to detail the specific acts that Hannah and Stuckless had inflicted on Kruze either separately or together between 1975 and 1982: "oral sex, anal sex, mutual masturbation, unwanted touching, fondling and kissing." The men also involved him in "group sex" with other boys. They told him that they had abused hundreds before him and were abusing hundreds more at the current time. They bragged about their exploits, pointing out the other boys they abused and telling Kruze how some of them had earned their nicknames. "They felt proud of their conquests," Kruze wrote. They also told him that he was their favourite, their number one boy.

Kruze went on to describe every spot where the abuse took place within Maple Leaf Gardens. He had even gone to the

Gardens and taken photographs of all of the places that still remained where Hannah and Stuckless had abused him, and photocopies of the pictures were now neatly identified and enclosed in the folder. George Hannah had abused him both in his office and in a vacant corner office near the Wood Street entrance to the Gardens, the very entrance where the head usher was posted and where the Maple Leafs players would enter and exit the building. Fans lined up at all hours to get autographs. What could the usher have been thinking, Kruze asked in his letter, when Hannah took him and other boys into the office for hours at a time?

Kruze wrote that most of the time Gordon Stuckless had abused him in the electrical room beside the east press box behind the grey section. There were several holes in one wall of the room through which Kruze could watch the games and concerts that Stuckless invited him to see. Stuckless also took him to a pornographic movie theatre just blocks from the Gardens and to a drive-in theatre, where he subjected Kruze to "kissing, oral sex, and mutual masturbation."

In addition to working at the Gardens, Stuckless was a substitute teacher for schools in and around Toronto, and he told young Kruze "ugly stories" about sexually abusing children in the showers at the schools. Stuckless also met boys on the team he coached for the Metro Toronto Hockey League; he had even been Kruze's coach for a year.

Hannah and Stuckless used "force and control," Kruze wrote, "and kept me in fear and silent." Stuckless would grab

Kruze's head, and he warned Kruze that if he told anyone what was going on, no one would believe him and he would just be hurting his family.

Kruze also pointed to John Paul Roby, an usher then still employed at Maple Leaf Gardens, as a "possible perpetrator." Hannah and Stuckless had told him that Roby was abusing other boys, and Kruze recalled that Roby had always tried to get close to him and rub up against him. Kruze also noted that Roby was always surrounded by young boys.

Kruze reported that he was writing to the police now because he was afraid that Gordon Stuckless and John Paul Roby were still abusing boys. And he was afraid that some of the boys who had been abused at Maple Leaf Gardens at the same time he was were now abusing boys themselves. "I have been told in therapy and in reading books," Kruze wrote in bold italics, "that minors that were sexually abused, have a greater chance of abusing. This concerns me."

Kruze's letter included a list of names, addresses, and phone numbers of employees of Maple Leaf Gardens who could confirm that he had spent a great deal of time there from 1975 to 1982, along with a similar list of boys he had seen during "group sex" or boys Hannah and Stuckless had bragged about abusing. Kruze added that he had even talked to a few of the survivors himself. Some of the men reluctantly admitted that they knew what he was talking about. "I believe there is still a lot of dysfunction at Maple Leaf Gardens," stated Kruze. "These people who are committing heinous crimes should be criminally charged and punished, and for all survivors at Maple Leaf Gardens, they should receive therapy paid by Maple Leaf Gardens."

Kruze ended his letter by pledging his help to the police: "I am committed to bringing justice to myself and hopefully to helping other survivors. Any help the police need, they only need to ask me and I will be there."

Tredrea was impressed with the work Kruze had done to present his allegations. He told Kruze that he and his partner would need some time to review the material and get back to him. In what seemed like no time at all, the most important meeting of Kruze's life was over.

Kruze was relieved. A huge weight had been lifted from his shoulders. He had finally done what he had set out to do so many times before. The police had taken him seriously. They believed him. That meant everything to him, but he didn't want to wait for them to get back to him. He wanted action now. He wanted Gordon Stuckless arrested immediately. Instead, he was told that he had to wait.

Days went by, and it seemed to Kruze that nothing was happening. He began to feel that everything he had worked so hard to prepare, every detail of his tormented life that was printed in his letter, was not being taken seriously. He feared that the attention he wanted to bring to Stuckless and his past crimes would not come fast enough.

Or, worse, what if nothing happened at all?

1

A Childhood in Hockey

Hi my name is Arnold Kruze and I live on 4 Howard
Dr. I have two brothers Ron and Gary, both of them
play sports. Ron plays school basketball and he is 18
years of age, and my other brother plays hockey for a
good team. Now it's my turn to talk. Well my age is 12
and I was born on April 22, 1962. And the same as my
brothers, I play sports too. Of course I play hockey for a
pretty good team and we're called the Toronto Redwings.
Most every day of the week we have some sports to do.
  —Arnie Kruze, 1974

IN 1974, ARNOLD MARTIN KRUZE wrote his life story for Room
7-6 at Bayview Junior High in North York, Ontario. (Arnie, as
he was called then, didn't start calling himself Martin until after
he turned thirty.) The blond-haired, blue-eyed boy wrote five
pages and covered the usual topics: family, early years, pets,
hobbies, and friends.

In blue ink and neat penmanship, he gave his older brothers first mention, then talked about his parents, who, he noted, were immigrants from Latvia. His father, he wrote, ran a drapery business, where he was "the boss," and his mother was "just a plain housewife" who helped out in the business from time to time. He added that "my mom just came back from USSR and she had the best time of her life."

Although Arnie said that he might need help with his spelling, he thought he would do well in English. He listed the sports he played when he had first attended Elkhorn Public School: floor hockey, soccer, and volleyball. He noted that his team had won the cup for house league "scoop" (or scoop-ball, a popular kids' indoor game) when he was in Grade 4, lost by one point when he was in Grade 5, and lost by a couple of points when he was in Grade 6.

His family didn't have any pets, but he thought that "all animals should be treated the same because an animal is an animal and they are just the same as me and everyone else." If he ever could have a dog, he would "love it so much." Under the heading "Hobbies," Arnie wrote that he collected stamps and leaves. Under "Friends," he wrote that he had a lot of them and that he would try to keep them, even though he was now in Grade 7 and wouldn't have much time to play.

He included pictures of himself as a baby in a carriage and at age twelve sitting on the bed in his room. There was one of his family, with a name and arrow pointing to each member, "and me the small one in the blue." There was also one of his house and front yard, with a note saying that the picture dated back to when the driveway was just getting paved. Arnie added another note at the beginning of his life story that he didn't want his pictures touched or taken.

Arnie's teacher corrected his spelling mistakes and gave his work a C but didn't offer any further comment. Almost any boy growing up in Canada during the 1960s and 1970s could have written a similar autobiography. Arnie's love of sports—especially hockey—and his after-school activities and hobbies, along with his admiration for his older brothers, made him like many of his friends and classmates. His sensitivity towards animals might have set him apart from some of his classmates, and his Latvian heritage would have distinguished him from "new Canadians" from other parts of Europe who were setting down roots in Toronto during this time.

The house pictured in his autobiography was like every other ranch-style house on his street, with an attached garage and big backyard. Compared with Toronto's downtown homes, which were built much earlier and more closely together, all of the houses on Arnie's street were spacious, separated by wide driveways and big front lawns. The neighbourhood was neat and tidy, projecting an aura of suburban middle-class success. Arnie's best friend, Kevin Crabb, lived around the corner, and Arnie spent hours playing at his house.

Arnie's mother, Astrida, came to Canada in 1948 at the age of twenty. She had endured the invasion of her country by Russian troops and had seen her own parents forced off to wartime camps in Siberia when she was only thirteen years old. Arnie's father, Imants, fought for the U.S. Army during the Second World War; even today, when he alludes to his wartime experiences at all, it is only to say that he knows too well what it means to be a survivor. In 1947, still a young man himself at twenty-three, Imants put the war behind him and made his way to Canada.

Astrida and Imants met and married in Canada. Imants worked tirelessly to establish and succeed in his own drapery business and by many accounts was demanding of not only himself but also his wife and, later, his children. He had great aspirations for them all and saw hard work, education, and good business sense as the keys to success. Arnie's parents also wanted their kids to take advantage of all things Canadian while at the same time fostering their connection to Latvian culture.

In addition to delivering the *Toronto Star,* collecting stamps, practising the drums, and playing organized hockey as well as after-school sports, Arnie, and his brothers before him, attended Latvian school on Saturdays and spent several summers away at Latvian camp. Gary had been named after a movie star, Gary Cooper, but Arnold was named after his grandfather back in Latvia; Arnie's older brothers teased him about his name. The family attended a Lutheran church in downtown Toronto and saw many of their Latvian friends there. Each of the boys had godparents and was confirmed in the church. When Arnie was a teenager, he played the drums for a Latvian show band called the Bobcats and dreamed of becoming a professional drummer when he grew up.

His parents' marriage had its ups and downs. Astrida was relieved when her husband was away from the house for long hours working. She felt that he was too tough on the boys and too tough on her. Imants, however, felt that he was forced to be the disciplinarian in the family because Astrida did not set any limits on the boys' behaviour. He also felt that even he couldn't discipline Arnie—the boy was always on the move and nowhere to be found when his father went looking for him. Imants would later say that he bore the brunt of all of the responsibilities for the family and that he tried to help his wife as much as he could. Astrida lived for her sons, and each day passed filled with the joys and challenges of raising them. To the other kids in the neighbourhood, the Kruzes seemed like the model family.

Although as a child Arnie Kruze couldn't have known how to describe his family in so many words, as an adult he would say that he "came from a very dysfunctional family." What Arnie didn't say in his autobiography was that he worried about his parents. He frightened easily and had a nervous tic. He was also afraid of his father's temper.

If there was ever an invention that could turn hardship and pain into freedom and pleasure—that could turn immigrants into Canadians and young boys into stars—it was hockey. In spite of any problems in the Kruze family—or perhaps because of them—Arnie, his brothers, and his parents were all crazy about the game.

For first- and second-generation immigrant families, involving their children in sports can be a point of entry into a new community. And hockey defines Canadian culture. Living a hockey life means that you belong.

It didn't take long for Imants Kruze to discover that in Canada hockey held a position similar to that of the arts in Latvia. And as fate would have it, one of his first friendships in Canada was with former Toronto Maple Leafs star goalie Turk Broda. Imants even shared an apartment with Broda in Toronto for a short time.

Imants also met Turk's brother, Lou, who was the general manager of ice operations at Maple Leaf Gardens for more than two decades. It was through Lou Broda that Imants later started to do business with Maple Leaf Gardens—he made all of the draperies for the offices, including the ones for then-owner Harold Ballard's office, and even for Ballard's home.

While Imants Kruze was becoming involved in the business side of hockey, Arnie was learning how to play the game. He learned to skate when he was about five, earlier than his brothers, and as a result he took to skating much faster than they had. Before long, Arnie was picking up the finer points of stickhandling and passing from Gary and Ron, sometimes on the ice of the local outdoor rink but more often on the driveway of the family home. Imants even constructed a net for the boys at his drapery factory: when the garage door opened, the net would swing into place, ready for the next game.

The brothers played hockey on the driveway seven days a week, with a big group of friends. They also got together with neighbourhood kids for road hockey games and tournaments.

According to Gary, "Road hockey was our life—it was the big thing. Dinner conversations were only hockey. We drank, ate, and slept hockey. That is what our lives were." Everyone in the Kruze family was happiest around hockey: at the rinks, practices, or games or watching the Leafs on Saturday night. "That was the best thing about our family dynamics," Gary says.

Their dreams were the driving force. Like countless other Canadian kids, the Kruze brothers and their friends might have been playing on the road and driveway and outdoor ice, but in their imaginations they were NHL stars like Guy Lafleur or Darryl Sittler or Ken Dryden, playing in front of screaming crowds at Madison Square Garden or the Montreal Forum, or best of all, Toronto's hometown shrine to hockey, Maple Leaf Gardens. Every breakaway and slapshot and kick-save took them another step away from the streets of suburban North York and closer to the Gardens down on Carlton Street.

Ron was the first of the Kruze brothers to play hockey in a youth league, but soon his love and talent for basketball had him playing on his high school basketball team instead. Gary went on to a successful career in minor hockey, progressing quickly from playing on local teams like Flemingdon Park at age fifteen to Willowdale Boys' Club (where he made captain) to a minor team called the Red Wings by age seventeen and next to a Junior B squad. He then stepped right into Junior A hockey, where he played for two years. Like many kids moving through the ranks of junior hockey, Gary dreamed of making a career of the sport. But only a very small percentage of

Canadian youngsters make it to the NHL or one of the other pro leagues in North America or Europe, and Gary lacked that extra measure of speed, skill, and size it takes to make the pros. He never lost his love of the game, however, and still competes in men's leagues today.

Arnie tagged along to all of his big brothers' games, and he too was a natural hockey player. As the youngest of the three boys, he had a pair of ready-made role models and coaches and thus developed his skills quickly. His parents drove all over the city to watch Arnie in games and practices. Imants made sure that the boys had the right equipment, though at least once that meant banging on the door of the local Canadian Tire store before it opened early on a Saturday morning, right before game time.

Arnie's first team, the one he joined at about the age of seven, was the Goulding Park Rangers, in the Metro Toronto Hockey League. Right from the start he was a goal scorer. And he was fast. Even though Gary and Ron were well ahead of Arnie in their own development, they could see that their little brother had talent. Arnie was always one of the top players on his team.

The following year, Arnie joined another youth team, the Dorset Park Bruins. Later he signed up for the Toronto Red Wings, which he wrote about in his autobiography. Now he was playing on real teams, even ones named after NHL clubs, like the Boston Bruins and the Detroit Red Wings, in real indoor and outdoor arenas, and, most significantly, under the guidance of adult coaches. Unlike pickup road hockey games, these contests adhered to the official rules of the game.

One season during his early years of junior hockey, Arnie scored fifty goals, and it didn't take his coaches long to recognize that they a special talent on their hands. It also didn't take Arnie long to realize that as one of his team's stars, he could start demanding special treatment. He demanded more and more ice time, and even threw the occasional temper tantrum if he didn't get the opportunities to play that he thought he should. Arnie was prone to occasional crying fits and outbursts of temper, which his family figured were the usual antics of a little brother with lots of talent for sports and an attitude to match.

By the time he was sixteen, Arnie Kruze was progressing up the ranks of junior hockey, much as Gary had. At eighteen, he tried out for Wexford Warriors Junior B (in the east end of Toronto), and by nineteen he ended up playing for Wexford Juvenile AA.

Throughout the boys' childhoods, Astrida and Imants would sit in their living room on Saturday nights and say, "Thank God that our boys are involved in sports. Thank goodness we know where they are. They are not in the malls, they are not doing drugs. They are watching sports or taking part in sports."

Hockey gave Arnie an escape from the problems at home and provided a way for him to feel good about himself. It also forged a bond between him and his brothers. It taught him about fair play, teamwork, and the rewards of hard effort. But Arnold Martin Kruze's relationship with sports was radically different from that of most kids, for his love of hockey was also fodder for manipulation and betrayal.

THIS CAN'T BE HAPPENING

IN 1969, WHEN ARNIE KRUZE was seven years old, Clifford Wright was seventeen and living in Hockley Valley, about 200 kilometres west of Toronto. His father had abused his mother and all of the children in the family. After she left and the Children's Aid took his sisters into care, Clifford and his brothers were left living with their father. When his best friend moved to Toronto, Clifford decided he had to get away from his father and headed there himself. Once he arrived, Clifford discovered that he had no way of tracking down his friend. Later, as he waited at the bus station for the bus to take him back home, he was approached by John Paul Roby, an employee at Maple Leaf Gardens.

> *He started just talking and being very friendly*
> *and seemed concerned, 'cause I was scruffy*
> *and ... I was hungry, and he asked if I wanted*
> *breakfast. I said, "I don't have any money, I can't*
> *buy breakfast."*
>
> *So he took me and bought me breakfast. He*
> *said, "You can't go home looking like that." So we*
> *went and he bought me new clothes, got my hair*
> *cut, and then we went to Maple Leaf Gardens.*
> *He showed me all around. Everybody knew him.*
> *I never knew his last name. They called him*
> *Johnny. Everybody, there was a couple of ushers*

there, and the players were practising and three or four of the players knew him by name and he introduced me to them. One of them was Carl Brewer and Dave Keon, I don't know who else.

I was in my glory, 'cause, like we were living in Hockley Valley and you never dreamed of going to Maple Leaf Gardens. It was just out of the question.... So, this is amazing. All I could think of was, "What do I tell everybody at home?" I never even thought to get an autograph or anything....

And then he said that he had to get his suitcase and so we went to his place—it was just around the corner from Maple Leaf Gardens—and that's when he said, "Well, you should pay me for what I've done for you."

I said, "I told you, I don't have any money." I still haven't clued in.

He said, "I don't want money."

And I said, "What do you want? I haven't got anything."

And then that's when he grabbed me by the crotch and he started to put his hand down my pants and I just froze. I didn't know what to do. All I could think of was, this can't be happening. I've been through this before, and it just can't happen again. And I started to step back and he said, "You owe me, you son of a bitch. You owe me."

And then he grabbed me, just like that, and I stepped back and his foot was on my foot and we both fell to the floor. It didn't take long to get away from him, because I was on the wrestling team at school, I was in all the sports, and I was in good shape, but I ran out of there so fast.

All the way home to Orangeville on the bus, I was just freaking out, and then as soon as I saw Pat [his girlfriend] I just fell apart. And I remember telling her some of the stuff that happened, I didn't tell her everything about him grabbing me by the crotch, but I told her about him threatening to kill me.

TRAPPED

At age 13, I was first introduced to Maple Leaf Gardens
by meeting the equipment manager at the time, George
Hannah, who was at a high level of management. His
age was approximately 50+. At 13 I am down there in
awe at meeting all the hockey players...going to the
dressing rooms...getting sticks, sitting up in the press
box. He made me feel like a 13 year old king.
  —Martin Kruze, 1994

THE SEXUAL ABUSE OF ARNIE KRUZE began as abuse does for so
many children: through a relationship encouraged by trusting
family members. The relationship itself was initially filled with
attention and kindness—the kind of interaction anyone would
want for a child. What makes sexual abuse so hard to recognize is that you don't know it has started until it is already too
late. By the time the ambush occurs, the trap has been set long
before and there doesn't seem to be any way to escape. What

made Arnie's abuse unusual was that it took place at Maple Leaf Gardens.

It is common knowledge that Maple Leaf Gardens is made of 750,000 yellow bricks; the fact that people know the number of bricks that went into the building's construction speaks volumes about its significance to Canadians. Hockey was the Gardens' most notable purpose, and the immortal announcer Foster Hewitt made sure that the thousands of Canadians who weren't there in person experienced it just the same. The building itself has had many nicknames over the years, including the "Taj Ma-Hockey" and "Puckingham Palace," reflecting its status as a shrine for Canadian hockey fans. Writer Charles Wilkins summarizes its place in Canadians' hearts this way: "The building's greatness was, of course, never primarily about bricks or accoutrements or functionality but about mystique, nostalgia and heroics—about the transporting quality of what went on there: events that inspired memory and imagination, that became history, and in some cases literature or even legend."

Despite all the lore that surrounds it, Maple Leaf Gardens is a pretty dingy place—it's an old building with dark hallways, ancient bathrooms, and dusty rafters. In contrast to more modern sports facilities like the Air Canada Centre, to which the Leafs relocated in early 2000 to play their home games, the Gardens is a dump. But therein lies a lot of its charm—it reminds people of pro sports of a bygone era. Maple Leaf Gardens was also the venue for all kinds of concerts, indoor track-and-field meets, and pro wrestling, and it was the home of Toronto's Junior A squad, the Marlboros, or "Marlies." Almost anyone growing up in and around Toronto has fond memories of their visits to the Gardens. For out-of-towners, it was always the place to visit because it was home to the Toronto Maple Leafs for sixty years.

Arnie's introduction to Maple Leaf Gardens came just as his brothers' had: through their father's friendship with Lou Broda. When Maple Leaf Gardens was being renovated and having new seating installed, Lou called Imants and invited him to come down and get ten seats from the red section. Thrilled to have their very own set of "reds," Gary and Ron, then aged twelve and thirteen, went down to Maple Leaf Gardens with Imants to pick up the seats. When they arrived to load them into the van, the boys met Lou Broda and some of the other Gardens staff.

Lou Broda knew how big a hockey fan Gary was, so he invited him to come down the next week to watch a game. He also told him to bring his skates. That night, Lou met him at the gate and showed him where to sit. When the game was over and everyone was gone, Lou told him that he could now have his turn to skate on the ice. Gary says, "I had the whole ice surface to myself for an hour. It was incredible." Broda told Gary that he could come down to watch a game anytime. His father just had to call ahead so that they could arrange to let him in.

Most often Gary went to the games alone, but Ron joined him for some and they both went to the concerts. Over the years Gary became such a familiar face at the Gardens that he got to meet the staff and some of the Leafs players as well. He was given hockey sticks used by Borje Salming, Darryl Sittler, and Bobby Hull, and he still has the sticks to this day. On one visit Gary met some of the police officers from 52 Division who played hockey at the Gardens on Tuesday and Thursday mornings, and they invited him to join their team. By age sixteen, Gary was going down to the Gardens all the time for hockey games and concerts and to play hockey with 52 Division.

Eventually Arnie asked if he could go along, and Gary took him to the odd game. One night when they entered by the side door, they ran into George Hannah, and Gary introduced him to Arnie. Maple Leaf Gardens had been Gary's home away from home, and now Arnie was becoming a part of it too.

George Hannah was equipment manager for Maple Leaf Gardens and for the Toronto Marlboros Junior A hockey team. Although he was in his late forties, he always seemed older than his age. He had grey, thinning hair and a pale face. His softspoken manner made him seem like a gentle, almost frail man. In his blue or brown suits, he was a fixture at Maple Leaf Gardens. All the boys coming through for Marlies games or to watch the Leafs practise would say hello to Hannah; he was someone to look up to in the world of hockey.

Hannah took Arnie on a tour and told him that he was welcome at Maple Leaf Gardens any time. He also gave Arnie a hockey stick.

Arnie and Gary made several more visits together. They met Leafs players and got autographs, and George Hannah continued to be an attentive host. The boys' parents never had any reason to question their trips to the Gardens because of the family connection to Lou Broda and because, after all, it was Maple Leaf Gardens, one of the most famous places in the country.

Two months later Hannah suggested that Arnie come down to some games on his own. What a perfect message for a thirteen-year-old to hear! His parents already allowed him to travel on the subway by himself, so there was no problem with his getting there. Being invited into the world of hockey and celebrities was better than being given the key to the door of a candy store—Arnie Kruze was in heaven.

George Hannah continued to take Arnie on tours; give him hockey pucks, sticks, and tape; and solicit autographs for him. He invited Arnie to sit in his box at Maple Leaf games on Saturday nights. On occasion Arnie even got to sit in the box of team owner Harold Ballard. To Arnie, George Hannah was Ballard's right-hand man. "You don't get to sit in Ballard's . . . private box at every game [during third period] if you are not somebody," Kruze later said. Even years later, after all that had happened, he couldn't help but exhibit the pride he had felt as a youth to be sitting in such an important place with such an important person.

Harold Ballard did not inspire good feelings in many people. As part of a triumvirate of owners that also included Stafford Smythe and John Bassett, he had purchased the Toronto Maple Leafs in 1961. Ballard ran his team like a tyrant, making most if not all of the franchise's business and on-ice decisions. In his personal life, Ballard was flashy and flamboyant, a crass millionaire with more money than good sense or manners. His profanity-laden tirades made great copy for the sports writers who covered the Leafs and his other team, the Hamilton Tiger-Cats of the Canadian Football League. In addition, he was continually fighting with his grown children over his various operations and assets, and his disputes with his girlfriend, Yolanda, who had legally taken the last name Ballard, were a source of public amusement. By the time of Ballard's death in 1990, the Ballard offspring and Yolanda were engaged in headline-grabbing squabbles over their inheritances.

None of Ballard's personal exploits meant much to Arnie Kruze, though. But he was impressed by George Hannah, who arranged guest passes to the games for him, his brothers, and his friends. Arnie felt even more important because he could flaunt his privileges to his brothers and his friends. Sometimes the passes wouldn't be there, even if he was told to expect them, but by this point Arnie was such a familiar face at the Gardens that he was admitted to the building without question. Arnie believed it was Hannah's power that made this possible. Whether or not George Hannah actually wielded such power, Arnie's belief that he did helped Hannah secure his admiration and trust.

Hannah began treating Arnie to dinners at the Hot Stove Lounge in the Gardens. Opened in 1963, the lounge was the first private club in a National Hockey League arena and was yet another way for Harold Ballard to rake in money. Toronto columnist Rosie DiManno describes the room as the "only vaguely plush environment within the Gardens... which has always felt to me like someone's drearily decorated rumpus room, with unimaginative cuisine to match." But the lounge was one of the few intimate spaces in the entire building, and along with its primary function as the deluxe dining room of the Gardens, it was used for press conferences and other important meetings. If you were somebody, you dined or conducted business there. If you weren't, you couldn't get past the door. There was no doubt in Arnie's mind: George Hannah was somebody. The maître d' and waiters soon called Arnie by name. If Harold Ballard was the king of Maple Leaf Gardens and George Hannah second in command, then maybe Arnie Kruze was its crown prince.

Hannah also took Arnie up Church Street to Gatsby's restaurant, which catered to the Gardens' faithful. Arnie's favourite meal was shrimp cocktail, Caesar salad, and steak. Arnie was especially impressed that the waiter prepared his Caesar salad right in front of him. It was over these dinners that George Hannah said he would help Arnie become a pro player. Hannah promised him a tryout with the Toronto Marlboros, which would be his steppingstone to the pros.

George Hannah was becoming like a father to Arnie—he gave him attention and provided him with the guidance he would need to find his way in the world of hockey. Certainly Arnie's own father had the same aspirations for his son, but he could never provide the access that Hannah could. Imants

Kruze was a committed father and vigorously encouraged his boys to stick with school and to work hard, but George Hannah also offered companionship and respect. Hannah always had time for Arnie, something that his own father had little of. It even seemed to Arnie that Hannah was comfortable letting other people think that he was his father. Since Hannah was more than thirty years older than Arnie, they didn't look too different from many of the fathers and sons who hung out at the Gardens.

As Arnie got older, it seemed to him that his mother didn't have much of her own life. With his father away at work so much, Arnie felt that he was taking care of things at his house, and he later wrote that he was like a husband to his mother. Arnie's brother Ron eventually couldn't stand living at home any longer and decided to move out.

Meanwhile, George Hannah had become gold to Arnie Kruze in ways that go beyond the access to hockey and celebrity afforded by Maple Leaf Gardens. If Arnie was feeling unhappy or neglected at home, if he was being made fun of or left behind by his older brothers, Hannah was there to give him attention and to provide everything that hockey had to offer. Father figure, attentive mentor, and hockey broker, George Hannah had become the centre of Arnie Kruze's young life. Hannah had set his trap.

The abuse began one day in 1975. "I remember the first time he sexually abused me like it was yesterday," Kruze would later reveal. "We were alone in his office near the Church-Wood Street entrance. George Hannah pulled out a porn magazine and showed me it—age thirteen, [in] 1975. We were looking at it, and he put his hand on my leg and started moving it up until he touched my penis. I was scared at this point and literally froze. He then unzipped my pants…and started playing with my penis. Then he unzipped his pants…and took my hand and put it on his penis. Then he started to have oral sex with me until I ejaculated in his mouth. He then grabbed me and started kissing me with his tongue in my mouth. He got me to kiss his penis for a moment, then we stopped and zipped up our pants. Then he took me up to the press box where I would always sit next to him."

What occurred that day in Hannah's office was an aberration of everything Arnie had experienced before. What began with Hannah's showing Arnie pictures of women's naked bodies, something that "men" do together, went haywire when Arnie himself became the object of Hannah's intentions. Arnie had been ambushed. This change in Hannah's behaviour was so shocking to Arnie that he froze. It was all he could do to follow Hannah's cues and demands. Being taken up to the press box after the assault was almost equally as shocking: Hannah was behaving as if nothing had happened.

Arnie could not understand what was going on. Until now, Hannah had been the antidote to everything that was wrong in Arnie's life and had offered everything that would lead to his future success. George Hannah was kind. He gave Arnie things and treated him like he was somebody.

Moreover, sex was something that men and women did. Although Arnie Kruze was thirteen at the time, not an adult like

George Hannah, and although he was attacked rather than asked if he wanted sex, Arnie's main fear was that this was what homosexuals did. One thing Arnie knew for sure: he hated it and he never wanted it to happen again.

But it did happen again, over and over. Hannah continued to invite Arnie down to the Gardens, and Arnie continued to go. He went hoping that what had happened in Hannah's office that day wouldn't happen again. He went because he loved life at Maple Leaf Gardens. He went because things were now so upside-down he didn't know what else to do. He went because he was scared about what might happen if he didn't go. "You aren't mentally developed like an adult to make decisions... you expect that people in authority and people you trust will make decisions for you," Kruze later wrote, "but when you get befriended and that trust gets broken it is very scary."

Hannah told Arnie that what had happened was Arnie's fault and that if his parents or brothers found out what he was doing they would punish him. Kruze wrote later, "He threatened me in a manipulative/aggressive way and to the complete reverse of a parental fashion of love and care." Hannah simultaneously treated Arnie as a son and a prince and as an object for his own use. Kruze recounted, "I didn't deserve to be treated as a piece of meat that you can tenderize, chop up, and eat. I was an innocent child of God."

Most often, children like Arnie Kruze are utterly alone when they are abused. The abuser finds a way to separate the child from others and creates situations in which the two are alone.

This way the child is the only witness. It also means that the abuser can more easily control how the situation is understood. For example, if an adult reaches over and slips his hand into a boy's pants, rubs his penis and then says, "Oh, sorry, I didn't realize what I was doing," it is likely that the child will accept the man's explanation, especially if he believes (and hopes) it won't happen again. If the adult tells the child his pants look too tight and reaches over to loosen them (while at the same time rubbing his penis), the child tends to accept that what the adult did was for him, and not for the adult's gratification. Being alone with someone who is usually bigger and older increases the terror and confusion that a child feels. He or she doesn't understand what's happening, when it will stop, or if the person is going to hurt him further. Even though a touch or kiss might not seem like actions that would hurt—though it may be done in a way that does physically hurt—the child is horrified that the action has taken place at all. The child is devastated at his or her very core. On the surface, some acts might not physically hurt, but the act of violation maims. The secrecy and silence that accompany the abuse further trap the child and make him or her feel complicit.

Arnie Kruze was most often abused alone by Hannah, but Hannah also brought other boys who worked as ushers or in other kinds of part-time employment at the Gardens together with Arnie for what Kruze later described as "group sex." When something like that happens, children still often feel alone and isolated because they don't understand what is happening.

Even as an adult, Kruze used the term "group sex" to describe what went on, but this term refers to adults who decide to have sexual contact with one another in a group, and it suggests that the participants are involved by choice.

When Arnie was nearly fourteen, George Hannah told him how much Gordon Stuckless, another employee at the Gardens, wanted him and then introduced him to Stuckless. The first time Stuckless abused Arnie was after watching him with a group of boys that Hannah had brought together in the vacant corner office. Hannah and Stuckless stood watching and masturbating while they instructed the boys to touch one another. Then Hannah and Stuckless joined in touching and kissing the boys. One of the tricks Stuckless used was to tell the boys they were going to play strip poker. According to the rules—and Stuckless followed the rules plus added a few more—if a boy lost a round, then an article of clothing had to come off or the boy would be told he had to touch another boy in a particular way. Boys brought together by one or two men who tell them and show them what to do are not having "group sex"—they are being molested in a group.

When the Metro Toronto Hockey League season began that fall, Gordon Stuckless became Arnie's hockey coach. Stuckless was very friendly and he was "a guy's guy." He was a skilled player himself. The boys on his team were always impressed with how hard he could shoot the puck. Arnie seemed to be one of the favoured players. He got all the ice time and was always in on the power plays. Gary Kruze remembers Arnie act-

ing up on the ice in ways that other coaches would never tolerate. If Stuckless told Arnie it was time to come off the ice, Arnie
would slam himself against the boards and refuse to come off.
Gary's coaches would never have put up with such behaviour.
Although both Arnie and his parents were happy that this new
coach was allowing him to play so much, the extra ice time had
a negative effect on his attitude as a player. Arnie expected the
same treatment from the next team he played on but didn't get
it. He got even more frustrated because the coaches didn't give
him the kind of ice time that he thought he was due. Arnie
thought that Stuckless had been rewarding him for being a
good player; he couldn't understand why his subsequent
coaches didn't operate that way.

George Hannah and Gordon Stuckless abused Arnie both
inside and outside the Gardens. Hannah took Arnie for rides in
his car and out to dinner near his apartment in Etobicoke,
where he lived with his mother. When she was not there
Hannah would abuse Arnie in the living room or in his bedroom. Hannah also sexually abused him during the car rides.
Gordon Stuckless's pattern was similar: he took Arnie for rides
in his car and took him to movies and to drive-in theatres. He
walked him up Yonge Street to see porn movies. The car rides
and the dark theatres gave Stuckless his opportunity to reach
over and grab Arnie's penis, and he would kiss him and masturbate him, or he would get Arnie to do the same things to him.

Even though Hannah and Stuckless both used their apart-
ments and cars to abuse Arnie and other boys, Maple Leaf

Gardens was a treasure house for this purpose. Hannah and Stuckless could invite Arnie and the other boys down to watch games, practices, and concerts, and they had access to offices (Hannah's office and the vacant office near the Wood and Church Streets entrance) and the electrical room. Stuckless even used the stairwells under the pretence of helping boys practise their shots—presumably the landings provided a flat surface for this purpose.

Whereas George Hannah tended to use his office to abuse Arnie, Gordon Stuckless took Arnie up to the electrical room behind the grey section. Maple Leaf Gardens is divided into five colour-coded seating sections—the golds (the arena's best seats, closest to the ice), reds, blues, greens, and greys (the seats farthest from the ice). Using the excuse that Arnie could watch whatever game or event was going on through several holes in the wall, Stuckless would take him to the electrical room and then reach into his pants and touch him, or he would kiss him and put his mouth on Arnie's genitals.

Hannah and Stuckless warned Arnie to stay away from John Paul Roby, who had been trying to hug and grab Arnie. They told him they wanted him to stay away from Roby because he was theirs alone. If Arnie told anyone anything, they would hurt him or his family. They even threatened that they would go to the police and tell on him. These threats made Arnie feel as though it was all his fault, that he was the one doing something wrong and that Hannah and Stuckless would do him the favour of not telling on him as long as he continued to cooperate. "I was like a pawn between George Hannah and Gord Stuckless," said Kruze years later.

Hannah and Stuckless built Arnie up and then cut him down, alternately bolstering and attacking his self-esteem. One moment he was the prince of the Gardens, sitting in Harold Ballard's box during third period; the next, he was being abused in the electrical room. Or he would be treated to an expensive dinner, then taken to the corner office at Wood and Church and splayed out naked on a blanket. At other times there would be no fondling or kissing and Hannah and Stuckless would give Arnie hockey souvenirs and reassure him that they were paving the way for his success in hockey. Arnie would never know what was going to happen next. Kruze would later say, "It [the abuse] was very scary, yet they built me up by giving me things—built my ego up and then deflated it with the coercion . . . which is very frightening. . . . So you don't know what to think. And they also romance you in a way. . . it's like a courtship . . . they treat you as something very special."

Every time Arnie went to Maple Leaf Gardens he believed that he was going to take part in things he loved. "When I was taking the subway down to the games and concerts I didn't think I was going to be abused . . . even sitting here I wouldn't think of that. . . . All I thought about was what I was going to see and the nice things I was going to get," Kruze recalled later.

The pattern continued for a long time. Arnie went to hockey games on Wednesday and Saturday nights, and he went to concerts on other nights. "George Hannah would be there before the game to get his hands on me," Kruze wrote later. "It was like his very own manipulative ritual. Before an event he would sometimes say that he couldn't get me in but [he] would come over to grab me and do his abuse, then pay me off." The same man who made it possible for Arnie to have complete access to Maple Leaf Gardens—with no strings attached initially—was now the man saying he wasn't sure if he could get Arnie in. Hannah's trap was tight. Arnie was more and more confused and unsure—he was going to be a hockey star (George Hannah told him so), and all of this was his fault (George Hannah told him that too).

At home Arnie would explode in fits of anger. Once Gary passed his bedroom and saw him having such a fit; then Arnie broke down and cried, "I just wish God would come and take me!"

At other times Arnie was depressed. He began to stuff himself with food, and he became disgusted with his body. He began to masturbate every day, and he sometimes felt that he wanted to cut off his penis. He cut classes at school. He felt that he couldn't get along with anyone. His only salvation during high school at Earl Haig Secondary School came from drumming in the school band and for the school show orchestra and choir. "I was never able to concentrate, feeling so separated from life and other students," he later wrote. "I missed hundreds of days or skipped off school because I was sickly depressed. I went from tutor to tutor, summer school to summer school." When Arnie finally completed high school, he cheated on his exams and tore up his diploma.

One wonders how Arnie's abuse could have happened at Maple Leaf Gardens and how it could have gone on for so long. Employees must have seen George Hannah and Gordon Stuckless entering all the various spaces with one or more boys time and again and then not coming back out for quite a while. Hannah frequently took Arnie into his office, where an usher sat right outside the door virtually all of the time. If someone knocked on the door, Arnie knew that he needed to hide or pretend that nothing was happening. Several Gardens employees who knocked on Hannah's door saw Arnie in the office with Hannah. Arnie's face would be flushed and sweaty, but they didn't say anything.

The era has something to do with it. In the 1970s, awareness about sexual abuse was limited. Many people thought it was something that happened only to girls. Families like the Kruzes would have worried more about a stranger abducting and molesting their children than they would about children being abused by someone they knew, such as a family member, neighbour, teacher, or coach. Children were told not to talk to strangers, who might be bad people. The idea was that if you didn't talk to them, they couldn't hurt you. Children weren't taught about sexual feelings, masturbation, same-sex and opposite-sex relationships, or comfortable and uncomfortable touch. Instead, they were warned against strangers.

How do you warn children about the person whom they or their parents already know and like? The same person who loves to horse around with kids and enjoys giving gifts? The person of whom everyone says, "He has a way with kids," and

"We're lucky to have him helping out" at the school, the community centre, or on a local team? On the one hand, this could be the behaviour of someone who genuinely cares about a child. On the other hand, it could be the behaviour of someone trying to gain a child's trust and cooperation in order to molest him or her. These same strategies are also used to build a relationship with the child's parent or parents in order to gain their trust and therefore more access to the child. If parents weren't aware of sexual abuse in general, they certainly didn't imagine their kids to be at risk in settings such as sports or school. And no one could imagine that it would take place at Maple Leaf Gardens. Yet it did go on, it seems, almost in public view.

Certainly, security at Maple Leaf Gardens was lax. Imants Kruze, who made the draperies for many of the offices, remembers that Maple Leaf Gardens was an "open building." Gary Kruze says that "in the Ballard years, it was very loose down there; if you knew anybody you could come in from the side door off Wood Street and Church Street. It was always, 'Oh yeah, you are so-and-so's friend, come in.' You would go to standing room, and you'd stand around for the first period and then you would look down and 'Oh, there's some seats in the golds, reds, wherever.' Then you'd take one of those seats for the second and third period. And I would say probably upwards of maybe four hundred to five hundred boys per game would have gone in that way, maybe more. There were kids in standing room, everywhere—standing in exits all the way around the rink. It got so bad that people had to fight their way through the exits to get to their seats, because all the kids were standing in their way." One year Harold Ballard sent out a memo to all the ushers and usherettes saying that nobody was allowed to stand under the exit signs. Since Ballard always sat in the box behind one of the end nets, the ushers did not allow anybody to stand in the exits within Ballard's view but they let the boys stand in all the other areas.

It is possible that the ushers who admitted so many boys so freely were for the most part doing it to reward eager fans for their love for the Leafs. Perhaps George Hannah, Gordon Stuckless, and John Paul Roby were the only three men who exploited the lax and friendly atmosphere at the Gardens to molest children. Clearly nobody made them accountable for their actions during their work hours. Were their activities supervised or monitored in any way? There seemed to be no restrictions on what they could do in the building. Were guest policies and admissions monitored? The many boys who hung out at the Gardens and crowded the entrances to the ice were not required to sit in designated seats. Was the behaviour of some of the staff, including Hannah, Stuckless, and Roby, ignored, quietly tolerated, or even sanctioned?

Many of the survivors interviewed for this book believe that the Gardens management knew what the three men were doing there but did nothing to stop it. Several of those survivors also claim that Gardens officials—including Harold Ballard—actually witnessed acts of sexual abuse taking place in offices and in the stands but did nothing to stop them.

Rumours circulated around Maple Leaf Gardens that some of the employees were "weird" or "queer." John Paul Roby's nickname around the Gardens was "bum blaster." It was okay to allude to unusual behaviour but not to do anything about it.

Had any of the boys understood what was happening to them and felt able or driven to tell, who would they have told? The boys thought George Hannah was senior management, and some knew that Gordon Stuckless and John Paul Roby were involved—who else was there to tell? If any of the boys did tell a parent or teacher, and if any reports reached management at Maple Leaf Gardens, what action was taken to investigate the reports and stop the abuse?

Once when Gary Kruze visited the Gardens when he was around twenty years old, George Hannah placed his hand on Gary's leg and then moved it up towards his genitals. Gary shouted, "What the fuck are you doing?" and smacked his arm away. Hannah replied that he was just being friendly. Shaken, Gary later decided to warn his younger brother about Hannah. When Gary told Arnie what had happened, Arnie assured him that Hannah had never tried anything like that with him. Gary put the incident out of his mind.

After nearly seven years, Arnie was abused for the last time on December 13, 1982. "There was a farewell concert for the rock band The Who and I wanted to take my best friend, Kevin Crabb, there," Kruze later wrote. "George Hannah said I couldn't get in because of the security and tickets were tight. But he made it clear that if I wanted to get in, I would have to pay the price." Arnie told Kevin to wait down the hall. Then he went into George Hannah's office and Hannah abused him. Kevin knew what was happening because Arnie had told him he had to pay for all his friends to come to concerts and hockey games for free. Afterwards Hannah asked Arnie to bring Kevin in, but he refused.

This incident was a turning point for Arnie Kruze. Until that day he had never fully understood the pact that he had somehow entered into with George Hannah and Gordon Stuckless. Even though Arnie knew on some level that he was being used to meet their needs, he thought he was "paying" for his and his friends' entry as part of his admission to the big league. The tickets, the privilege of sitting in Hannah's and Ballard's boxes, the equipment, the kindness, the attention, the threats, and the promises now stood out for what they were: instruments of manipulation. When Hannah asked Arnie to bring his best friend into this pact, it finally hit him full on: Hannah was using him. He wasn't a player—he was being played. Now Hannah wanted Arnie to recruit a new participant. Hannah's and Stuckless's tricks had worked for seven years, but now Hannah had gone outside the familiar realm that Arnie had come to tolerate. He had finally gone too far.

As Kruze himself said later: "George Hannah tore my life into pieces, causing me so much pain and destruction that I wanted to die as a child while I was being sexually abused and molested. George Hannah stole my childhood, teenage years and adulthood. For which the love for life, myself and others and the trust of people and adults was shattered."

I'M STILL TRYING TO FIND OUT WHAT THE HELL WAS GOING ON

BRIAN SILBER KNEW Gordon Stuckless from everywhere.

> *I mean, there was the 600 Club [a boxing club],
> there was the school, Regent Park School, and as
> a kid I went to the school, I went to the 600 Club,
> I went to where they had the swimming pool in
> Regent Park, I played floor hockey. In all these
> places, I was abused and with Gord as well. He
> controlled Regent Park basically, as far as sports or
> anything goes. You know, boxing clubs. Like I
> said, [he] took me to the school, introduced me to
> people, and then abused me in the basement.*

Brian was also abused at Maple Leaf Gardens, in different sections, at different times, by different men. It seemed to Brian that each man had his own section. He lists off his abusers:

> *There's Gord, there's George Hannah, and there's
> John Roby, and there's Ballard, you know. And
> Ballard didn't touch or anything, but he knew and
> he watched.*

Brian remembers Roby saying, "Don't let Gord know that I got you in here." He has at least one image locked in his mind that haunts him to this day: being abused in front of Harold Ballard's desk, while Ballard sat behind it.

John Paul Roby would place him in a particular seat in the red section.

> *He placed me about six rows up from that pole or whatever in the reds and there'd be people sitting right beside me, and he'd use me as his little boy or something. And fondled me and stuff while the game was going on, and I sat there so scared, you know, yet I kept going back, because I wanted that plaque [with the original six NHL hockey team pucks]. And I wanted to find out what the hell was really going on. I'm thirty-four now, and I'm still trying to find out what the hell was going on.*
>
> *You can't even imagine what that does to the spirit, my body as a kid standing there so alone in such a big building, and people there, cops there, this is when the game's going on, shit was going on. And it's like, "Help, cop, I'm here, this is happening," and nobody's doing nothing about it. I remember sitting behind the glass, here's the net, I was sitting in the seats here, and he comes by and does his thing and people sitting right next to*

us, man. And Ballard in his fucking window up
there, just looking all miserable down at us, and
I just sat there and I let it go on.

Manny DeSousa was born in Portugal and came to Canada when he was three years old. When he was fifteen, his parents told him he had to stop going to school and start working to support the family. His first job was at Maple Leaf Gardens, where he was sexually assaulted by George Hannah in the Toronto Maple Leafs dressing room.

They [other employees at Maple Leaf Gardens] say
they didn't know it was happening. They knew, as
God is my witness, they knew this was going on.
They used to joke about it. The foremen used to
joke about it. "There goes George, there goes the
gearbox [Hannah] with another little boy. Heh,
heh, heh." "Oh, there's George with another little
boy. He's gonna give him a hockey stick. . . . "
They knew about it, just didn't care. Nobody
cared. Nobody gave a shit about me. They didn't
care about anything except making money. That's
all they cared about. . . .

   He [Hannah] wore a suit and he worked directly
for the Toronto Maple Leafs. He had grey hair, he
was losing his hair. He looked like he couldn't
hurt anybody . . . until he made his intentions clear,

I had no idea. It was like getting hit with a shovel upside the head. I was molested by a cousin of mine when I was nine years old, and I actually saved my brother from getting molested. I thought, "Hey, I come from a tough family." I never seen it coming.

It happened in the Toronto Maple Leafs dressing room, after he was talking about sexual things. He told me he was going to call the police and get me charged for the things I was stealing. I said, "You gave them to me." He said, "I didn't give you anything."

Where I come from, how I was raised, you just take your lumps and you move on. "Be a man."

I never told anybody because I was ashamed. I was fifteen years old. I used to struggle with whether I was homosexual or not. . . . Absolutely I thought George Hannah was gay afterwards; then, no, but afterwards, for sure. . . . I thought he was a big faggot. I shouldn't even be saying he's a faggot. He's a rapist is what he is.

Until I moved out, I had the [hockey] gloves that he gave me. I don't know why I kept them.

I tried to laugh it off. I tried to pretend it didn't happen. I was very upset. I was very bitter. After it happened I was so angry. And I was angry too that I couldn't tell anybody. I couldn't tell my mom.

When I got molested by my cousin, my mom told me I must have liked it if I let it happen. So there you go, that gives you a good sign that I couldn't go talk to my mom. Who was I fooling? Nobody really. I wasn't even fooling myself because I knew it happened.

When that happens to you, it kills your soul.

3

THE DOWNWARD SPIRAL

There are demons chasing this man.
—Diana Roman, 1986

WHEN ARNIE WAS SEVENTEEN, Hannah encouraged him to have sex with other men. At first this was confusing to Arnie, because Hannah often talked about sex with women, even though he also bragged about his conquests of other boys. The fact was that Hannah had a foul mouth and talked about sex all the time.

Hannah convinced Arnie that he should go to the St. Charles Tavern, a gay bar just up Yonge Street, not far from the Gardens. Hannah told him that the men there would love him. Arnie was beginning to think that his sexual experiences with Hannah and Stuckless might have caused him to be gay, so Hannah's encouragement started to make sense to him. Still caught in Hannah's trap, Arnie went to the St. Charles Tavern and to other gay bars as well.

Throughout his late teens, Arnie became sexually involved with gay men in their late twenties. Much as he had been passed from Hannah to Stuckless, he was now passed from one gay man to another, sometimes in the same night and the same bed. In an interview much later with the Toronto journalist James Dubro, who was writing a piece on Kruze for *Saturday Night* magazine that was never published, Kruze said he liked the attention but not the sexual experiences. He considered having sex with men to be a form of self-punishment.

Kruze realized years later that when Hannah encouraged him to go to gay bars, his goal was to promote Arnie's involvement in gay sex. If Arnie Kruze was gay, then George Hannah wouldn't have to believe that he had molested him. Instead, Hannah could tell himself that he had simply introduced Arnie to the gay life that he was already headed for.

Arnie became obsessed with sex in all variations. He continued to masturbate every day, often so many times that he would hurt his penis. Arnie devoured endless porn magazines and often went to strip clubs. Even while he was sexually active with gay men, he was zealously pursuing heterosexual experiences through pornography and strip clubs. He went to a massage parlour on Yonge Street, near Maple Leaf Gardens, and at least once to a female prostitute.

At age twenty, like his brothers before him, Arnie left home. He moved into the basement apartment of a house owned by his brothers on Browning Avenue, in the Riverdale area of Toronto.

Although his mother seemed to be doing better, Arnie was worried about leaving her on her own with his father. He identified strongly with his mother, believing that they were both sensitive and easily upset. He was critical of everything his father did. About a year after Arnie moved out, his mother came to realize that she had been living a nightmare and that she had only survived because of her sons. Now that all three boys had moved away, she realized that it was time to leave Imants. So she moved in with Ron, who by this time had married a woman named Nanette and now owned a house on Fulton Avenue, just a block north of where Arnie was living with Gary.

Arnie got along with both of his brothers. He especially admired Ron, who was working in their father's business and had always been a ladies' man. Arnie considered Gary more old-fashioned, but Gary had opened his own textile sales agency and Arnie believed that he was on his way to success. Compared with his brothers, Arnie felt that he had made a mess of his life, and he began to feel more depressed than ever. He couldn't sleep at night and often felt exhausted in the morning. His body felt "strange," but he couldn't figure out why.

Arnie went to see his family doctor, who referred him to a psychiatrist at the Clarke Institute of Psychiatry—now known as the Centre for Addiction and Mental Health—a large mental health research and teaching facility that provides in- and out-patient treatment. Arnie told the psychiatrist that he felt he was thinking a lot about killing himself. The doctor wrote that a man had "seduced" Arnie when he was thirteen and that he was feeling guilty about the relationship and that he blamed himself for his past life. Arnie also became upset when he talked about his parents' relationship. The doctor prescribed antidepressants, and Arnie agreed to return in two weeks. After seeing the psychiatrist several more times, he didn't feel the need to return.

In April 1983, when Arnie had just turned twenty-one, he started a new job as a bus boy at Hemingway's restaurant in Toronto's tony Yorkville area. He still wanted to be a drummer, but he needed a job to support himself in the meantime. Previously he had worked in sales for both his father and Ron, but he always resented the control his family held over him and his income. This would be his first full-time job away from family connections. Arnie worked hard at Hemingway's and the customers liked him. Within a couple of months he was promoted to waiter, and later he became the manager. In August 1984, while Arnie was working at Hemingway's and feeling good about himself, George Hannah died. Flags at Maple Leaf Gardens were lowered in his memory.

One night after Arnie had finished working, he headed over to a club in Yorkville to hear Platinum Blonde. There he met eighteen-year-old Diana Roman, who had won a set of tickets to see the band perform. A student at Humberside Collegiate, she had never been to a bar before and was wearing a turtleneck so that she would draw as little attention to herself as possible.

Diana was sitting at the bar with her girlfriends when Arnie came over to meet her. Diana thought he was sweet, almost nerdish, and that made it seem safe to exchange phone numbers with him. The next day he sent her roses, and her fairytale romance with Arnie began.

Except for the way he dressed—in clothing that seemed out of date and didn't match—Arnie seemed to do everything right: he wrote Diana love notes and sent her cards. He picked her up at the library when she was finished studying. He was supportive when her parents split up. Arnie also told her that she had led a sheltered life and that he was going to show her what she had been missing. She decided that she would teach him how to dress better; she didn't know that he dressed the way he did to make himself look unattractive because he didn't want people to notice him.

Diana was also flattered by Arnie's extravagant attentions. He would pick her up in a limousine and take her to a fancy restaurant, and champagne and flowers were a part of every occasion. Arnie took Diana to Gatsby's and ordered Chateaubriand for two. If a band was coming to town, Arnie would call down to Maple Leaf Gardens and find out which gate they should come to, and they would enter with no questions asked. He told Diana that he had worked there at one time (apparently he did receive two paycheques for helping Stuckless move some equipment), and she was impressed with his connections. "Arnie was a player," Diana says.

Arnie was playing out his relationship with George Hannah. He never told Diana anything about Hannah or Stuckless, but

he became obsessed with her in the way he later believed
Hannah was obsessed with him. Arnie lavished gifts and dinners on Diana as George Hannah had lavished them on him.
When he took her to Gatsby's, Kruze realized later, it was the
"same insanity repeating itself." What came across as caring and
support to Diana was Arnie's single-minded devotion to her. He
doted on her much the same way that Hannah had doted on
him. He didn't do it because it felt right, he did it because he
felt compelled to do it. He began to run up his credit cards. His
job at Hemingway's could not support the lifestyle he was lead-
ing. "I spent money like it was water," Kruze said.

He was also becoming increasingly fearful of people and
places, and Diana represented safety. If Arnie focused all of his
attention on her, he wouldn't have to deal with other people.
He never told Diana that he was disgusted with his own body
and wanted people to stay away from him, that he felt empty
and worthless.

Arnie had periods of depression, which his brothers told
Diana about, but she didn't have any understanding of what
was going on. No one did. To Diana, Arnie just seemed to be on
the go, trying out different things and never feeling satisfied
with anything. One day Arnie got up and decided to completely transform his bedroom: he decorated it in peach and
black, a look that had been made popular on rock videos and
concert T-shirts at the time. He hung pictures of Diana everywhere. The next day he was on to something else.

Throughout much of their nearly five-year relationship,

Diana attended the University of Western Ontario and lived in London, Ontario. She and Arnie wrote to each other and saw each other on weekends. Diana believed that one day she would marry Arnie, and he finally did propose to her at Hemingway's, after they had been together for almost four years. She said yes at first, but by the next day she had changed her mind. She wanted someone with a plan for the future, and Arnie's plans kept changing.

Months later he proposed to Diana again. This time it was over Chateaubriand at Gatsby's, and this time she said yes and meant it. Arnie now had a plan for the future; he was going to work with his brothers in the window-covering industry. But Diana continued to feel uncomfortable that Arnie seemed to make plans and change them all the time. If he was working towards a goal and something got in the way, he would drop the goal. Diana believed that if they were married and they hit any problems, Arnie would bolt rather than stay to work them out.

In addition, Arnie seemed to be overly interested in sex. He liked to talk dirty to Diana about sexual encounters and had ideas about engaging in group sex with men and women. When they went on holiday together to the Dominican Republic, Arnie seemed obsessed with looking at other women. Diana began to worry on a very practical level: What if Arnie carried out some of his sexual fantasies? AIDS was new and was killing people, and she was afraid that he would get AIDS and so would she. It started feeling too risky to be with him. Diana wanted stability, and things were becoming less and less certain. Once, in his sleep, Arnie sat up with a start and screamed, "No! No!" and then lay back down. It was at this point that Diana knew, "There are demons chasing this man."

Diana was only seeing the tip of the iceberg, however. Every day Arnie woke up thinking about sex. He wanted it all the time. He also had mixed feelings about sexual intimacy. As much as he wanted to be intimate with her, the physical closeness scared and confused him. He didn't know how to behave. He was convinced that if Diana ever found out the full extent of his obsession with sex, she would leave him. Later Kruze said that he only enjoyed sex if he was using his partner, and then he felt guilty and ashamed. So, instead, most of the time he focused on the other person's needs—he was just an object to be used.

Within a few months Arnie told Diana he was ending the relationship because he wanted someone who was more experienced and who was farther along in her career. Weeks later he came to her door and begged her to marry him and become the mother of his children. He pledged to her that he had changed and promised her the future she had been wanting.

Another time he came back insisting that she needed to be saved; he had found God and could help her. Diana knew, once and for all, that there was something terribly wrong with Arnie. Again, she told him that the relationship was over and that he should take what he had learned into his next relationship.

Towards the end of his relationship with Diana, in 1987, Arnie returned to his family doctor and was referred to a new psychiatrist. Arnie was depressed and feeling like a failure, and he continued to feel that something physical was happening to his body. Sometimes he felt there was someone with him when there was no one else around. He thought constantly about being in car accidents and dying. When he was driving, he imagined smashing into a guardrail or the railing of a bridge. He told the psychiatrist about his past worries about his parents and about what the psychiatrist described as his "sexual activity" as an adolescent. Arnie told him that he always felt different from other people.

By October 1987, when he was twenty-five, Arnie's life had become unbearable. He was working in Ron's business, and Ron told him that he wasn't working hard enough. His father was pressuring his sons to take over his drapery business and threatened to sever his ties with Arnie and his brothers if they didn't. Arnie was obsessed with his body. He believed his thighs were too big, and even though he was working out all the time to keep himself in shape, it didn't seem to have any effect. Arnie believed his genitals were evil and thought about taking a knife and cutting them off. Even though he believed on some level that God was not a punishing god, he felt that he had sinned and was being punished just the same. Arnie Kruze was spiritually, emotionally, physically, and mentally bankrupt.

He decided that the only thing he deserved in life was to die. He took about a hundred extra-strength Tylenol and thirty antidepressants and washed them down with alcohol. After swallowing the pills, he called his brother Gary to tell him what he had done. Gary called an ambulance and rushed over to be with him. When he arrived, Astrida, Ron, and his wife, Nanette, were already upstairs with Arnie. As he was being wheeled away, Arnie shouted out that he tried to kill himself because of what George Hannah had done to him. All four family members were stunned.

Arnie spent two days in intensive care at Toronto East General Hospital with his mother sitting by his side. He believed he had almost died, but he reassured his mother that he was too chicken to ever kill himself. He was then transferred to the psychiatric ward at North York General Hospital for several weeks. "I thought I was crazy," Kruze wrote later. Arnie felt better almost immediately, and even though he had a long list of complaints, he insisted that he was ready to leave. He wanted to get his life back on track and to work on his career as a drummer.

Arnie had also decided that he had to give up on his relationship with Diana once and for all after he blurted out his past to his brothers and his mother. He had only told them that he had been abused one other time, when he got very upset and frustrated and shouted that they would never understand what he was going through. Arnie became convinced that Diana now knew what had happened to him, and he wondered how she could love such a terrible person. But Diana didn't find out about Arnie's suicide attempt or about his past until much later. The only message Arnie gave her about ending their relationship was that he wanted someone with more experience. As vulnerable and embarrassed as Arnie was feeling, he had kept his secret from Diana and had told his family little more.

Within only a few weeks, Arnie was worried and depressed

all over again. Once again, he believed that he didn't deserve to live. This time he got into his car and drove to a bridge. He considered jumping over the side, but he stopped himself and returned home. When he told his brothers what he had done, they insisted on taking him to the hospital. They urged the doctors to admit Arnie, but he refused to stay and returned home. Later that night he decided to see how high he could get, so he overdosed on more of his prescription pills. Arnie ended up back in the emergency room at North York General Hospital that same night.

Throughout 1988, Arnie saw his psychiatrist off and on and continued to take antidepressants. He was now over his suicidal feelings and was working once again as a waiter at Hemingway's and at another restaurant called Chandlers. But his obsession with sex intensified. Diana had wished him well with his next relationship—but it turned out that his next relationship would be a series of encounters with call girls.

By his mid-twenties, Arnie had become, by his own admission, a sex addict. He went from woman to woman. Believing that prostitutes were the only kind of woman he deserved, he began using escort services. In a six-month binge, he spent $10,000 to $15,000 on call girls because he wanted to have the best escorts. He also continued his tradition of buying expensive dinners and gifts for women—both call girls and regular dates. And he had unprotected sex because he believed that he deserved to catch a fatal disease and die a painful death. Diana's fears about Arnie's risky behaviour were coming true.

Around this time Arnie also started using crack cocaine, and before long he was addicted to it. Crack took care of all of Arnie's unbearable feelings and thoughts. He later called it "another way to punish myself and maybe force an overdose heart-attack." His addiction to sex and drugs became combined with two more obsessive/compulsive addictions—overspending and bingeing on food. Just as his salary at Hemingway's couldn't support his lifestyle with Diana, it couldn't sustain his spending on crack cocaine. Once again he ran up debts and maxed out his credit cards. Arnie appealed to his mother to help him, and Astrida spent several thousand dollars to pay off his debts.

The more Arnie needed money to support himself and his addictions to drugs and sex, the less able he was to hold down a job. Arnie first quit his job at Hemingway's in 1986. He returned there several more times to work as a waiter but ended up quitting after about six months each time. It seemed to his family that every time Arnie got his life together, it would take about six months for everything to come crashing down again. At one point Arnie went for a job interview at a new place. His future boss invited him up to his cottage for the weekend to wrap up the deal. Arnie fled, believing that this older man was going to sexually abuse him. In between his restaurant stints, Arnie also worked again for his family, this time selling fabrics for Gary's company.

In September 1990, Arnie's pain and terrible feelings overwhelmed him again. His sex drive was out of control. He felt

guilty about using escort services. The women he dated casually kept telling him that the only thing he had on his mind was
sex. Again he tried to commit suicide by taking an overdose of
prescription pills, aspirin, and alcohol; he called 911 and again
was taken to hospital by ambulance. This time Arnie stayed for
five weeks. He participated in individual, group, and family
therapy (with Gary, Ron, and Nanette) and made "reasonable
progress." He talked about his finances and relationships as failures. Arnie told the doctor that he had been molested at the
age of thirteen, and the doctor then recorded that Arnie "went
through a homosexual period of 4 years from age 13–17."
Arnie was treated with medication and discharged.

Throughout much of his contact with hospitals during this
time, whenever Arnie reported that he had been "seduced" or
"molested" as a youth, the doctors invariably wrote that his
relationships with Hannah and Stuckless were homosexual.
The doctors did not see Arnie as someone who had been victimized by substantially older and more powerful men. Instead,
because the sexual contact was between two males, it was characterized as "homosexual." Any woman reporting that she had
been "molested" or "seduced" as a thirteen-year-old by a man
would have been viewed as a victim of abuse, not as being
involved in a heterosexual relationship.

Between September 1990 and May 1991, Arnie tried to kill
himself three more times: he slashed his wrists, climbed up and
sat on the ledge of the Bloor Street Viaduct, and overdosed on
more pills. He also continued to use crack. Throughout this

time Arnie wanted to die more than ever. Gary wrote Arnie a
letter entreating him to believe in himself and to pray to God to
help him overcome his anxiety and negative thoughts.

Arnie was in and out of the psychiatric ward of the Toronto
East General Hospital. He was becoming well known to the
department. He was described as having a "severe borderline
personality disorder, a lot of it resulting from sexual abuse at
the age of thirteen to nineteen and coming from a very severe,
dysfunctional family." Hospital staff were working with Arnie to
get him into Homewood Sanitarium in Guelph for an assessment. Arnie believed Homewood could help him, but if he
wasn't accepted there, he wanted to try a group for sexual abuse
survivors that he had heard about.

For the first time, Arnie was hearing himself being described as someone who had been sexually abused. At times he
felt hopeful about his future. Other times he slept for sixteen
hours a day, unable to get out of bed to perform the simplest of
tasks, although he was still constantly in pursuit of a release
for his uncontrollable sexual urges. He went to stay with his
mother from time to time because he felt safe when he was
near her.

In March 1992, Arnie went to the Golden Valley Health
Center in Golden Valley, Minnesota, where he finally began
receiving what he called the "specialized treatments and therapy" that he believed he needed to begin his long journey of
healing. At the center, Arnie examined the relationship between
his childhood and experiences with sexual abuse and his cur-

rent problems. For the first time he began to understand what effects it had had on him as a child to be scared of his father and depended on by his mother and to be manipulated by adults to meet their needs. He understood that being treated this way had overwhelmed him and left him feeling worthless. He attended twelve-step programs and developed strategies to stop his negative thoughts and change his behaviour.

Finally, Arnie was getting the help he needed, but it was a struggle to go to the clinic—both financially, although Ontario health insurance was helping fund the stay there, and emotionally, because it meant acknowledging and confronting his problems in a concrete way. Upon his release, a month later, he returned to Toronto. As much as Arnie wanted to overcome his problems and as helpful as the focus on his abuse and addictions had been, he became flooded with memories and feelings about George Hannah. He couldn't face them and went on a three-month binge of using crack and seeing prostitutes.

In December 1992 Arnie decided to attempt another thirty-day program to address his compounding problems. He also made another decision. When he arrived at Founders Hall Fairbanks Program in Vermont, he arrived as Martin Kruze. From now on he would be called by his middle name. He never wanted to be referred to as Arnie or Arnold again.

Even with his resolution to change his name, Martin was still in despair. He wasn't suicidal, but he was afraid, lonely, guilty, ashamed, remorseful, and depressed. His counsellor wrote, "His greatest fear is not to recover and the pain of recovery."

MY FATHER WOULD HAVE KILLED HIM

ILAND AKBAR ATTENDED Park Public School after his family immigrated to Canada from Turkey. Gordon Stuckless became his gym teacher and hockey coach.

> *He'd walk around with a Maple Leafs jacket on;*
> *he was somebody I looked up to. He knew I was*
> *fascinated with hockey, he knew I was fascinated*
> *with him being a member of the Maple Leafs*
> *organization. He was proud to walk around the*
> *way he was. To this day, I can never stop thinking*
> *of the way he would show me how to use the stick*
> *and the puck. He had such skill that I thought he*
> *was going to make me an NHL player. He could*
> *drill the puck; when he shot it, it was like*
> *it was going to go through a concrete wall. I*
> *couldn't even lift the puck up.*
>
> *The only thing that my father ever told me was*
> *to always cover myself, because of our religion*
> *[Islam]. So I was the only child in the shower with*
> *underwear on, and [Stuckless] noticed that a few*
> *times. One particular day, he came in and started*
> *making fun about that. All the other kids started to*
> *laugh and they're all walking around naked, but*
> *he got everybody's towels in his hand, and he'd*
> *walk into the middle of the shower room and say,*

"Jump for it," and he'd throw the towels up and
the children would have to try to grab their towels
before the towels landed on the ground and got
wet. I can't ever get rid of his face. That laughing,
evil smile and all the children jumping, you know.
He was observing us.

I never knew what to call my privates. I never
knew. We didn't have sex education then. And
he'd place his hand underneath and he'd start to
grab and squeeze and, I guess, I mean just fondle
me. Maybe I was stupid, but I didn't know.

One time, Stuckless arranged to meet Iland at the Gardens
so that the boy could see a game.

I got home right after school, and I told my Dad. I
said, "Bubba, . . . is it okay if I go to the Gardens,
'cause he's [Stuckless] going to bring me in?" And
that was a game day. When I ended up getting
there, there was a whole bunch of kids there. And
he came to the door. I know he couldn't see me
directly, he saw other kids, but he looked around.
He stepped outside for a little while and he said to
me, "Come on in. I've got to get you something."
And when I came in . . . he goes, "I can't do noth-
ing with you now, everybody's in the building and
everything," and he handed me some pucks with

the Leafs logo and a little tiny hockey stick and he goes, "I'm sorry, all the other kids, the people in the building—just tell your Dad we'll do it another time."

I got back home . . . and the pucks were on the table, and my dad was all happy. "You're going to get the chance, that's why I brought the family to Canada, so you guys could have a chance." I explained things to him. I said there was a bunch of kids there, but he didn't want to get the kids upset or something like that. I'm talking in Turkish to say these words. He didn't want to get these other kids upset and he didn't want the other bigger people to know. But I said, "Look, Dad, this is what he gave me anyway." And my father was just very proud that somebody was taking care of me. Now I know Stuckless was taking care of me in his own little way. If I had told my father [that Stuckless had abused him], I know . . . I'd have been the first to be dead, and when I say dead, I mean dead, not a beating, dead. And I know my father would have killed him. My father was a very strict man, a very strong man, and he would have killed him.

THE FIGHT FOR SURVIVAL

*I need a lot of help. This is a life and death situation. I
choose life. George Hannah killed me once and I won't
let him destroy me any longer.*
—Martin Kruze, 1994

IN THE EARLY 1990s, Martin Kruze found two people to help
him in his fight for survival. In May 1992, at a conference on
sexual abuse, he met Toronto lawyer Susan Vella, who specialized in sexual abuse cases for the firm of Goodman and Carr. As
he talked to her, Kruze began to think about how he could turn
his life around. In subsequent meetings and telephone calls
with Vella, Kruze decided there were five things he wanted.

First, he wanted to heal from his abuse. His visit to the
Golden Valley Health Center had started him on the road to
recovery, and he needed to keep on this road until he was
healed. Second, he wanted to stop the cycle of abuse that he
was convinced was still going on at Maple Leaf Gardens. Third,

he wanted criminal justice: Gordon Stuckless needed to be held responsible, and he needed therapy to help him deal with what he had done to Martin and the other boys. Fourth, Martin wanted financial justice—compensation for his seventeen years of "pain and utter hell" and all of the financial losses he had suffered by not being able to stay employed or pursue a career. Finally, Martin Kruze wanted to raise public awareness about sexual abuse. He wanted the other boys abused at the Gardens to have professional help, he wanted other sports organizations and corporations to know that sexual abuse could be going on, and he wanted parents to stop letting their children go to places where they could be abused. He resolved that if he could stop one child from being abused, all his efforts would be worth it.

Martin Kruze had set out a tall order for himself. Soon he met the second person who could help him accomplish his goals. Kruze began to see Toronto therapist Jim Dickinson for therapy once a week beginning in November 1993. Kruze wanted counselling with an expert on sexual abuse and childhood trauma, and he believed that Dickinson was the right person for him to work with. Dickinson typically charged about $100 per session, but Kruze was not able to pay. Dickinson agreed to treat him anyway; Kruze would apply for funding from the Criminal Injuries Compensation Board of Ontario—a body that awards money to successful appellants who have experienced losses as the result of a crime—to cover his treatment expenses.

Kruze had another idea that became increasingly attractive

to him: What if he were to sue Maple Leaf Gardens for what had happened? Winning such a suit would meet a couple of his objectives. Maple Leaf Gardens would be forced to admit that abuse had taken place on its premises and it would have to ensure that it didn't happen again. Further, he would be compensated for his suffering and the money would solve his desperate financial problems.

On January 19, 1993, Susan Vella sent a registered letter marked "privileged and confidential" to Cliff Fletcher, president and general manager of Maple Leaf Gardens, Limited. She told Fletcher that she was acting for Arnold Martin Kruze regarding a pending action concerning "multiple incidents of sexual assault and sexual abuse" that had occurred at the site of Maple Leaf Gardens. The letter named George Hannah and Gordon Stuckless as the chief perpetrators, and it listed the acts inflicted on Kruze and the dates and places they occurred. The letter stated that George Hannah "illicitly induced" Kruze to engage in acts of sexual assault and sexual abuse in exchange for various privileges, such as free passes to hockey games and concerts and free hockey equipment. The acts of abuse included "oral sex, anal sex, mutual masturbation, unwanted touching, fondling, and kissing." The letter also stated that Kruze was only one of a number of boys who were induced into having group sex with Hannah and "other employees of Maple Leaf Gardens." Vella stated that as a result of the abuse, Kruze "suffered from intense and extreme psychological and emotional trauma which has often had physically damaging side effects."

Kruze's position was clear: Maple Leaf Gardens was liable for all the damages that he had suffered as a result of the abuse because it occurred on the premises of the Gardens. The Gardens had failed to provide a "reasonably safe place for children who were invitees, contractual invitees, and, in Mr. Kruze's situation, a one time employee." The letter claimed that Maple Leaf Gardens was liable "for breach of fiduciary duty owed to the children who attended at Maple Leaf Gardens events; and is also vicariously liable for the unlawful acts carried on by Mr. Hannah who had then the position of Senior Management and who was allowed to manipulate corporate benefits for illicit purposes as above described."

Stressing that her client was motivated by the desire to have any form of abuse at the Gardens stopped once and for all, Vella stated that Kruze had instructed her firm to begin legal proceedings "to obtain compensation and to seek relief which will ensure that the sexual assaults and abuse stop at Maple Leaf Gardens, Limited." Vella said that Kruze would be willing to avoid "the unpleasantness of the public nature of legal proceedings" if Maple Leaf Gardens would be willing to settle out of court for $1 million. Vella concluded by asking for a response within three weeks.

The Gardens management did not agree to the proposed deal, and over the next many months Kruze and Vella built their case against Maple Leaf Gardens. Kruze began assembling the material that was needed. He wrote out the names and addresses of all of the therapists, psychiatrists, and other doctors who had treated him over the years and asked them to release copies of his medical files to him. He returned to Maple Leaf Gardens to interview employees who had been abused along with him in the 1970s and 1980s. He obtained the addresses and phone numbers of others who no longer worked there so that he could contact them. He spoke with one of the victims who had been abused in a group with him. This man agreed to meet with Kruze's lawyer and to act as a witness.

Later, Kruze returned to the Gardens with a camera and photographed all the places where he had been abused. Kruze was meticulous in his work, developing lists of what George Hannah and Gordon Stuckless had done to him and describing how they had tricked and manipulated him. He listed the names of the other victims he knew and of employees he believed had witnessed—or should have realized—what was going on. He knew them so well that he listed their positions beside their names: captain usherette, stickboy, trainer, maintenance worker, and so on. As Kruze collected the details of his life and talked with Dickinson, he came to understand how he had been manipulated by Hannah and Stuckless and how he had been living out the effects of his abuse. For the first time in his life, Kruze was developing a picture of what had happened to him.

But filling in the details was a painful process. He began attending support groups such as Alcoholics Anonymous and Narcotics Anonymous. He moved into a house for people recovering from addiction problems. The government subsidized his rent, and his only source of income for much of this time was welfare. He got a job selling shoes but lasted only six days because he couldn't handle the stress.

Pulling together all of the information that would become the evidence for his case against the Gardens gave him a purpose. As much as it hurt, he hoped that delving into his past would take him further along in his recovery. Kruze wrote messages to help himself: "My healing process has started. When I write my feelings of the past abuse and the overwhelming life I have had, sometimes I want to run and hide, but I know I am a Survivor and this will be a lifelong process that I have to deal with on a daily basis so my life doesn't destruct."

Several telephone calls and meetings took place between Vella and the lawyer from Borden & Elliot, which represented the insurers for Maple Leaf Gardens, Royal Insurance. Unsatisfied that any progress had been made through those contacts, on December 23, 1993, Kruze instructed Vella to initiate legal proceedings. Vella filed suit number 93 QC 46434 with the Ontario Court of Justice, General Division, naming Kruze as plaintiff and Maple Leaf Gardens, Limited, as the defendant. The suit was filed in the amount of $1.5 million, sought in compensation for the Gardens' alleged negligence, occupiers' liability, and breach of contract and fiduciary duty, and included $500,000 sought for "special damages and punitive damages."

"It was reasonably foreseeable that children and adolescents would be present at MLG for various events," clause number 25 of the suit reads. "It was further foreseeable that these children and adolescents, being in a class of individuals who are peculiarly vulnerable to sexual abuse by persons placed in positions of trust, power and authority over them, were vulnerable of being sexually abused."

A series of communications took place between the lawyers and their clients for the next twenty-three months. Martin became increasingly anxious. Nothing was happening fast enough—sometimes it took weeks for the lawyers to even reach each other directly. Every step that went beyond a simple communication took months. By October 1994, Kruze and Vella had secured most of Kruze's medical records, and they assembled them into a "two volume medical brief" for review by Borden & Elliot. Six months passed before that review was completed.

In the meantime, Kruze applied to Ontario's Criminal Injuries Compensation Board for compensation as a victim of a crime. He was able to use much of the same extensive documentation about his abuse and health history that he had collected for his claim against Maple Leaf Gardens. He also asked Dickinson to write a report on his condition, and Dickinson agreed.

"For years Martin has not been succeeding with his life task. He has escaped life and has been so seriously drug addicted as to be life threatening. Martin was at a very high risk of suicide," wrote Dickinson. "Martin's journey to adult life and health has been fraught with failures congruent with an individual who had been so sexually violated. As of this date, Martin is again on the path of recovery and has been drug/abuse free for a month." Dickinson concluded that Kruze needed an intensive program of therapy, composed of thrice-weekly sessions, "possibly for life" and certainly for a minimum of three years.

In February 1995, two members of the compensation board, David English and Linda Abrams, found in favour of Martin Kruze and awarded him $17,000 plus $500 to cover legal expenses. "In making this award," English and Abrams wrote in their judgement, "the Board recognizes that no amount of money adequately compensates victims for the injustices that they have suffered but also finds that quantum of the award to be reasonable within the context of the Act, and generally in keeping with other Board decisions for incidents of comparable nature and severity."

For Kruze, the award was the first official vindication that he'd been wronged. Given his continuing financial and psychological stress, the settlement was a relief.

In August 1995, Vella received a telephone call from the lawyer acting for Maple Leaf Gardens. The Gardens was prepared to settle for $25,000. Since Kruze's initial demand was for $1.5 million, he was deeply offended by the offer. Vella responded that in light of his severe trauma and the expense of past and future therapy, her client could not accept the offer. The suit was taking such a toll on Kruze, however, that both lawyer and client believed that it needed to be brought to a conclusion as soon as possible. Vella made a counteroffer of $60,000 and the Gardens agreed to pay Martin Kruze that amount.

The agreement had strings attached, of course. In addition to cancelling his suit against the Gardens, Kruze was asked to hold the organization completely blameless for what had happened so many years before. He could no longer say, at least officially, that Maple Leaf Gardens was at fault. If he did, he would have to return all of the settlement. Kruze was not allowed to speak about the terms or circumstances of the agreement, or even about the fact that the settlement existed.

Like the abuse he had endured years before, what had just transpired between Kruze and Maple Leaf Gardens was to remain a secret, "other than as required by legal process." In other words, a legal investigation could require Kruze to reveal information, but otherwise he could not say anything. "It is the intent of the parties to avoid and prevent publicity regarding the circumstances and the terms of this full and final release."

Martin Kruze had sued Maple Leaf Gardens, and, in effect, he had won. But he'd achieved very little of what he had set out to do. Tracking down and compiling all of the information had given him a purpose and helped him deal with his overwhelming feelings. He understood better the many ways in which he had been exploited. But Maple Leaf Gardens paid him off in petty cash, compared with what he had been seeking. It was humiliating to accept that all of his pain was valued at $60,000.

Still, given all of his financial problems, Kruze must have felt that although the award was much less than what he'd hoped for, it was still a lot of money to put towards his debts. And he'd taken on the big boys and proved that he could follow through on something until it was done. He'd gotten Maple Leaf Gardens to admit—at least to him—that enough serious wrongs had taken place on their premises that he was owed something. To Kruze, the settlement meant that the Gardens' management was taking some responsibility for what two of their employees had done to him. And he could rest assured that his efforts would have helped ensure that other children would not be abused at Maple Leaf Gardens, because the Gardens would surely now act on his complaint by firing any other possible offenders and improving their security system.

Spending money he didn't have had been a long-standing problem for Kruze, but now he had it to spend. The settlement caused friction in his family. The last thing he wanted was for them or anyone to try to control what he did with the money. Such control represented everything that had happened to him at Maple Leaf Gardens. It seemed to Kruze that no one in his family told him how wonderful it was that he had received this money and that his abuse was being acknowledged. He believed that all his family was interested in was trying to protect him from spending the money.

With $60,000 in his pocket, Kruze went about settling some old debts. He paid the money he owed to both of the people who had become so central to his recovery, therapist Dickinson and lawyer Vella. And he spent a considerable portion of the settlement on a flashy car and on drugs.

Right after he received the settlement, Martin also called Gary and invited him out to dinner and a Maple Leafs game. He made it clear that he'd be paying for the whole shot. But instead of sitting in the seats that Gary figured Martin would be able to afford, they sat in expensive seats in the gold section, close to the ice. The dinner was lavish, too. "I kept wondering, 'Hey, can you afford this?'" says Gary. "And he was saying, 'Yeah, sure, no problem—this is all on me.' It was kind of like his way of getting back at the Gardens."

But returning to the scene of his abuse was, on the surface at least, a strange thing to do. Why would he subject himself to even one more trip through the doors of Maple Leaf Gardens? No doubt, Kruze was still psychologically tied to Maple Leaf Gardens in what is often referred to as a "trauma bond," in which the victim of abuse becomes emotionally and psychologically bonded to the offender and other aspects of the abuse. George Hannah was gone, Gordon Stuckless no longer worked there, and yet Maple Leaf Gardens—the symbol of Canadian pride and the place that he loved (and despised)—still held Martin Kruze. He was once its up-and-coming prince. He had been somebody there, even if everything had been resting on a house of cards built by Hannah and Stuckless. But Kruze was gutsy. He, Martin Kruze, had taken them on. If watching hockey is what he had always loved to do as a kid, why wouldn't he place himself right back in hockey's epicentre? He couldn't get hurt there anymore. He was an adult now, able to come and go like everyone else; no one was controlling his actions there but him. Maple Leaf Gardens was still the place to be and now he was there, treating his brother and smiling to himself like a satisfied cat.

I Felt Hopeless

IN 1987, WHEN MARTIN KRUZE tried to kill himself for the first time, Gordon Stuckless was abusing Darryl Bingham, who was growing up in Richmond Hill, Ontario, just north of Toronto.

> I don't know when he [Stuckless] showed up, just all of a sudden he showed up at the arenas and he started off coaching—and he was really outgoing. Always playing with the kids, always willing to take them to movies and to a Leafs game, just a bunch of little things, and it all seemed fine. He was good friends with my father. He coached with my father. He stayed over in our house at night. He came over for Christmas dinner one year. He spent time with my grandmother, our whole family, and everyone in the neighbourhood enjoyed him being around. He used to get us into the school where he worked in Oakridges and we played floor hockey and basketball, whatever games, and played on the computers, and he was known as a great guy.

Things changed on the first night of a hockey tournament in Trenton, Ontario. Darryl was expected to sleep in a cot in his parents' room and Stuckless's room was across the hall.

*I remember we were playing hockey in the hall-
way that night and . . . I don't know if my parents
went to sleep first or whatever, and I just said,
"I'm going to stay in Gord's room." Okay, no problem. And that night, I remember we were watching
TV pretty late and I fell asleep and Gord was
reaching over and he started to grab me and put
his hand down my pants. I was awake, but I didn't
turn around. I didn't. I felt hopeless, really—well,
not hopeless, more like I wanted to run or get out
of there. I knew it wasn't right. 'Cause, that's all I
ever heard . . . you know, if anything ever happens,
if you're ever in any trouble, like, don't let people
do this to you, don't let people do that, but, at the
age of thirteen, I didn't know what this man was
going to do, if he was going to hurt me. . . . I didn't
know what he was going to do. He always came
across as someone who could take care of himself.
He would wrestle with you and grab your inner
thighs, and always press his thumb in certain
areas, where it hurt. I was afraid that he would do
something to me, so I didn't say anything to him,
I didn't turn over, I just laid there and ended up
going to sleep. And in the morning, he said,
"Sorry," and I played dumb, as if I had just been
sleeping all night, and I said, "Sorry for what?"
And he goes, "Oh, you know, what I did last*

night. I'm very sorry and I don't know why I did it and it won't happen again." So I figured, he's never done this before. . . .

And I don't think it was too long after that that his father passed away, and my father and I attended the funeral, just showing you how close we were, how much respect we had for him. What happened that one time—I thought it was done with. Then a few months later. . . a couple of friends and I were invited by Gord to go over to the school and we were playing on the computers, and I was having a few problems. Gord was in the staff room or something, but there was also a little first aid room, or a storage room, and there was a couch and a chair there, and I asked him for help, and he goes, "Oh, it's going to cost you" and looked at me, and I knew what he meant. Like, I just knew. So, I turned around, and he goes, "No, come here." And again, I could have run, sure, but, it's not a kid's responsibility. . . . And he called me over and that's when he undid my zipper and had oral sex with me. And, then he did my zipper, my pants back up. I just stood there in front of him, not knowing what to think. Then I went back and played with the computers. And on the way home, he dropped everybody else off first. Nothing happened on the way home, but the whole way home I was trying to tell him, "That's it, never touch me again." But I couldn't say it. And, like, I knew it was wrong, and I couldn't say it to him. I tried so hard, I don't know if I didn't want my father knowing, because he was his friend. I never, ever thought that my parents wouldn't believe ... maybe I thought, this is my problem. Because I knew it was wrong.

And that night, I went into the house, and my mother was just around the corner at my grandmother's and I didn't want to tell my dad because it would hurt him. I'm sure my mother too. But this was a friend of my dad's and so I went over to meet my mother and I was trying to tell her the whole way home—it's not even a five-minute walk—and I couldn't. We were in the driveway, and I stopped there and I said, "There's something wrong. Gord's been touching me." And she just started crying right away, and after a little while, she asked me, "What do you mean? Like how?" And ... we went inside and I went to my room and my mom went in and told my dad what I was telling her. And, right away, he grabbed me and put me in bed with my mom, saying that I wasn't to be alone, he didn't want me alone. And I believe he went to one of his friends' houses, and then he went to the police.

5

MARTIN KRUZE BREAKS THROUGH

*Hi, my name is Martin Arnold Kruze. I was a 13–20
year old minor, a child, a victim of sexual abuse and
sexual molestation at Maple Leaf Gardens from years
1975–1982.... These were the Harold Ballard days.
Maple Leaf Gardens was a sex haven for pedophiles,
from executives to ushers to all the victims, minors and
precious little boys. Maple Leaf Gardens... when are
you going to wake up? It frightens me that nothing
appears to have changed at Maple Leaf Gardens.*
—Martin Kruze, 1997

THINGS WENT WELL FOR A FEW MONTHS after Kruze received
his settlement. He kept up his therapy with Jim Dickinson, and
he got a sponsor who would help him with the twelve steps of
Narcotics Anonymous and support him when things got tough.
He attended meetings, kept a journal, and focused on getting
better. But all this still didn't seem to be enough.

Soon Kruze ran out of settlement money. The satisfaction of winning his suit wore off. All of the work that he had done to gather the evidence for his case was finished, but what did he have to show for it? No justice, no acknowledgement, no apology—and Gordon Stuckless was still free. Kruze was feeling more and more that his silence had been bought—just as it had been bought twenty years earlier. The real problems of his abuse, and the abuse of others at Maple Leaf Gardens, had not been dealt with. No amount of personal work was going to bring Stuckless to justice or make Maple Leaf Gardens truly accountable for what had happened there. But right now, Kruze had to focus on keeping himself alive. He borrowed money from anyone and anywhere he could get it, and he used it to buy crack. Crack highs meant that he disappeared for several days and that he didn't have to deal with his feelings and memories.

But he also worked casually, driving for a limousine company and acting as an event manager and waiter at parties and receptions for a catering company called Actsent. One night in 1995 he found himself working with an attractive woman named Jayne Dunsmore. He was drawn to her sparkling blue eyes and ready smile, but at first he found her standoffish, since she was more concerned with serving food and drinks than with getting to know him. A dynamic woman with many years' experience in catering and selling specialty food items, Dunsmore was starting up her own catering business and she worked for Actsent in the meantime.

Martin and Jayne saw each other at a few more catering

affairs, and one night on a break they went out and sat at a picnic table, where they talked about their families. After that Jayne started looking forward to seeing Martin at other events. Unlike many other men, he expressed his feelings and seemed to be genuine. He was also good-looking, and she liked his dry sense of humour.

One night when Martin came to work he didn't look well. He left early and on his way out gave Jayne his phone number. He also told her that he would call her, but she didn't hear from him for more than six months.

During this period, Kruze lived in several different places: for a time with his mother, then with another girlfriend, and later with other members of the Cocaine Anonymous program—yet another program he had joined. Martin could get support and validation at any of the twelve-step programs he attended. All such programs are modelled after Alcoholics Anonymous, and unlike programs run by professionals, they have no admission requirements, time limits, or reports. The only requirement is that participants have a desire to stop their addiction. Because addicts relate to each other's experiences, they can help each other get clean. Support and inspiration are available at round-the-clock meetings. Still, Kruze believed that he needed intensive, professional help, so he also attended treatment at a drug rehabilitation centre near Ottawa. Ron drove him there and stayed over the first night to support him.

One day, Martin arrived back in Toronto and called Jayne just as he had promised. By coincidence she was giving a party of her own that same night and she invited him to come. At the time, Jayne was living with her mother in North York just blocks from the house where Martin grew up and played hockey in the driveway.

He arrived at precisely seven o'clock, dressed in a suit and bearing a bottle of wine, though he wasn't drinking alcohol himself at that time. Martin knew other people at the party, but he followed Jayne around "like a duck." After the party ended, he sat with Jayne and her mother talking on the couch. When he left, in the early hours of the morning, he told her that he would take her out for dinner in the new year.

What started at the picnic table months earlier continued at the subsequent dinner. Over four hours, Martin told Jayne all about himself, his life, his abuse, and his addiction to cocaine. It seemed important to Martin that he tell her everything. He wanted her to know all about the person she was becoming involved with. Jayne was impressed by how frank he was and by how well he was doing—he had been free of cocaine for four months and was on the road to good health. Because of his shocking past and his sunny disposition—and the contrast between the two—Dunsmore found Martin unlike anyone else she had ever known in her life.

Soon Martin and Jayne were falling in love—but Martin hesitated to make any sexual advances. It was almost as if he were an adolescent, unsure of what to do next. He seemed most interested in talking with Jayne. He also used to write letters and tell her what he was thinking and feeling about their relationship. He would tell her about his fears and how he wanted things to go. "It was just so charming," Jayne says. "I'd never met anyone like him."

They decided to go to Mexico for a holiday together. Martin's sponsor from Cocaine Anonymous was not in favour of the trip; there wouldn't be meetings available for Kruze to attend for support, and it would likely deepen his involvement with Jayne. The sponsor didn't object to Jayne herself, but he feared that any intense relationship would be a distraction from Kruze's focus on his own work. Martin's parents and brothers, however, were thrilled to see him so happy in a new relationship.

Although Martin was anxious about his sponsor's concerns, he was almost giddy with excitement about going away with Jayne. The trip would become one of the high points of their relationship—except for one incident. When they were staying in Puerto Vallarta, resting by the pool, Martin reached over and took a sip of Jayne's drink. Jayne assumed that Martin had picked up her drink in error. But Kruze had done it deliberately, and he became upset with himself for violating his pact not to drink or do drugs. He began to berate himself and became cold towards Jayne. This was the first time that Jayne had seen him behave this way. His reaction was so extreme that he seemed like a completely different person.

As Jayne got to know Martin better, this ugly part of him would return from time to time. She and Martin referred to this part of him as "Arnold"—the part of Martin that would emerge when, Jayne says, "Martin would start feeling bad about himself. Arnold was the person who Martin fought his whole life, internally, this person who said, 'You're no good, you're a piece of shit, so go smoke dope, you know, you're not worth it, nobody will love you, your family hates you, you're not doing any good in this world.' "

Jayne could also see how much of an influence Ron and Gary continued to have on Martin. Their concern about his mental health and his financial problems came across as anger and criticism. In Jayne's view, Martin was the scapegoat for everything that was wrong with the family. She sat with Martin and wrote a long letter to Astrida, Gary, and Ron explaining this point of view. As far as Jayne was concerned, they were part of what was keeping Martin sick. But the family no longer knew what they could do to help—they'd tried everything, and nothing seemed to work.

Martin began to see his father more and to appreciate all he had tried to do for him. His father had been a successful businessman and had taught him his basic business skills. He admired his father's accomplishments and was happy to see him in a new marriage with a woman who Martin believed was good for him.

Throughout their relationship, it seemed to Jayne that Martin would go into cycles of depression almost every four months. He worked to keep his negative feelings about himself in check, but then he would start doubting himself and feel like killing himself. Every four to six months, Martin would also disappear for a few days at a time, and it wasn't until later that Jayne discovered he was going off to use crack. She tried to be supportive by not intruding too much into his life, but it was not easy.

Jayne rented a tiny basement apartment on Lonsdale Road in Toronto's Forest Hill area, and in 1996 Martin moved in with her. It became their love nest. Once Martin filled the apartment with balloons to celebrate Jayne's birthday. He would go to great lengths to show his love for her, but he always discouraged her from doing the same for him. He didn't feel comfortable receiving gifts, so she gave him cards telling him how lucky she was to have found him. They both believed that God had brought them together.

In January 1996, Martin Kruze returned to Maple Leaf Gardens to see a hockey game. He saw John Paul Roby working there, as well as men who had been abused when he was. Kruze felt sick. Nothing had changed at Maple Leaf Gardens. The only person he didn't see there was Gordon Stuckless, but all that meant was that he was abusing boys somewhere else. Kruze realized that he was not going to conquer his abuse as long as Stuckless was free. He wanted everyone to know what Stuckless had done to him and hundreds of other boys and he wanted him behind bars to punish him and to keep him away from other boys.

Kruze vowed that he would bring Stuckless to justice. But what if no one believed him? Maple Leaf Gardens had not taken him seriously. They had paid him off with petty cash, and it was now obvious to him that they hadn't done a thing to make sure the abuse stopped. Otherwise, what was John Paul Roby doing still working there? Roby had never abused Kruze, but he had tried. What were the other men doing there? They were victims. Maybe they had become abusers and more children were being abused at Maple Leaf Gardens. The victims needed help, Kruze needed help, and Maple Leaf Gardens didn't care. Bringing Stuckless to justice became his new purpose. That would get their attention.

He got out his files to see if he could go to the police or if the settlement with the Gardens prevented him from doing so. The agreement said that he could not disclose anything to do with the settlement, "other than as may be required by legal process." He contacted Susan Vella and told her that he wanted to go to the police. It soon became clear to him that once he identified Stuckless to the police and they conducted an investigation, the story would become public if Stuckless was arrested.

Kruze was prepared to do everything he could to get Gordon Stuckless. But he also had to make a living. He never seemed to have any money, and Jayne felt that she was carrying all of their financial burdens. She had opened her catering business—A Culinary Affaire—and together she and Martin worked to build its clientele. Martin also applied to participate in a small business development program. He couldn't stand being dependent on Jayne and wanted to open a business making, packaging, and selling hors d'oeuvres and sandwich wraps, which he believed could be successful. But he also needed to pursue Gordon Stuckless.

When Jayne and Martin weren't working on their business

plans, they worked on Martin's letter to the police. Martin wrote out everything he wanted to say by hand, and then Jayne typed it for him. He had to be careful, and everything had to be in order. Most of all he had to overcome his sick feeling that he wouldn't be believed and that he would lose his last chance to stop the abuse.

On January 7, 1997, NHL player Sheldon Kennedy named Graham James, then a coach with the Swift Current Broncos in the Canadian Hockey League, as the man who had been sexually abusing him since he was a young player. This announcement was unprecedented on a national scale. In contrast to the step that Kruze would soon take, Kennedy waited until Graham James had been convicted before he spoke to the media. When he did, he identified himself as someone who had been sexually abused throughout his adolescence. His pain and isolation had been so great that he wanted other survivors to know that they were not alone in their experiences.

Kennedy was the first professional hockey player to go public with this kind of revelation. Given the atmosphere of pro hockey, it is not farfetched to think that he might have been rejected by the fraternity of pro players for admitting to his past. But Kennedy felt he had nothing to lose—for everything had already been lost years earlier. Kennedy also made it clear that his abuse was widely known throughout the sports community and among members of the media. There had been jokes and teasing for years in the locker rooms. And yet everyday Canadians had had no idea what had happened to him or that sexual abuse was a risk associated with hockey.

Kennedy's disclosure was the jolt Kruze needed to get himself down to the police station and through its doors. Still, it took several weeks of attempted trips and checking and rechecking his materials to get himself absolutely ready. On January 24, 1997, Kruze finally made it into the station. As relieved as he felt after he met with Detectives Dave Tredrea and Blair Davey—who seemed to believe him and to care about what he had to say—he was frustrated that nothing happened immediately after his visit. It was just like dealing with Maple Leaf Gardens and the civil suit all over again.

But Tredea and Davey had begun the investigation. After consulting with Toronto's head Crown attorney about the allegations against Stuckless, they invited Kruze back in for a formal interview. Because historical sexual assault is difficult to prove, they said, they would not be sent to the east coast, where Kruze believed Stuckless was, without some supporting evidence.

On February 4, feeling hopeless, Kruze wrote a letter to his father that he never mailed. He wanted him to know that he loved him, that he was happy they had repaired their relationship, and that he hoped one day he and his brothers would have the same respect and love for one another again. He said he hoped he would see his father in heaven and signed the letter Arnold Martin Kruze.

On February 10, Kruze wrote a letter to his brother Gary's wife, Teresa Kruze, then a popular anchor on TSN, commending her for her sensitive coverage of Sheldon Kennedy's disclosure and asking for information to enable him to contact Kennedy.

Martin wrote, "At this point, I can't disclose any details of my personal sexual abuse and sexual molestation from ages 13–20 because my situation is currently under a police investigation. My personal police detectives who are working on the case told me there is a chance the media will get hold of this because any investigation is open to the media and is public knowledge. That's out of my hands. I put that in God's hands. I would greatly appreciate, from the bottom of my heart to yours, receiving the address of Mr. Sheldon Kennedy. . . . This I ask of you, not just as a reporter, but as a family member, the wife of my brother. This is very important to me. This is one of my ways of healing." He wanted her to respond before she left to cover the Blue Jays' training camp in Florida for two weeks.

Somewhere in all of this he got so scared and overwhelmed by everything that he began to doubt himself and believed, once more, that he should kill himself. Martin Kruze again attempted suicide on February 13. No one seems to know exactly what happened, however, because the only record of his attempt was a police report. Neither Gary nor Jayne knew anything about it.

Two days later he was back at his campaign. He contacted Dale Brazao of the *Toronto Star* to tell him that he had been to the police and that it was only a matter of time before Gordon Stuckless would be found and arrested. He gave Brazao copies of everything: his letter to the police, his statement of claim against Maple Leaf Gardens (with the amount blacked out), the lists of everyone he believed knew something about or had experienced the abuse, the precise locations where the abuse took place in the Gardens, photos of himself playing hockey, letters from his therapist and his minister, the letter he sent to his sister-in-law, and so on.

Finally Kruze heard from Tredrea again. Unbeknownst to him, Tredrea and Davey were out following up on the names listed in Kruze's materials. Many of the men questioned denied that they had ever been abused, but some admitted that they had. Kruze's hard work was paying off. However, the police were not optimistic about locating Stuckless—especially if he was in Newfoundland.

Once again, Kruze decided to take matters into his own hands. This time, he'd play detective. "Nothing ever happened fast enough for him," Jayne says. Kruze started tracking down old hockey contacts, and call after call led him to a phone number in Toronto. Kruze tried the number, and a young girl—who, Kruze later said, sounded as though she was about twelve—answered the phone. Kruze told her that he was an old hockey buddy of Gord's and that he needed Gord's address in Newfoundland so that he could invite him to a reunion. The girl replied with surprise—Stuckless wasn't living in New-foundland; he was right nearby, in Scarborough. Sure, she'd be happy to provide his address and phone number so that Kruze could contact him.

With this sleight-of-hand and a few phone calls, Martin Kruze had done something the police had not been able to do. He had found Gordon Stuckless. After reporting this information to the detectives, Kruze learned that Stuckless would be arrested at eight thirty the next morning.

Kruze called Dale Brazao and updated him on the day's events. He wanted to believe that once the media picked up the story they would never let it go. But he couldn't simply leave it in one reporter's hands, so he called Ben Chin, a crime reporter that he knew at Toronto's City TV. Then he called his family and friends, along with Jayne's, because he wanted to make sure that they heard it all from him first. According to Jayne, "He wanted everybody to know what had happened to him in his life. And he didn't want anybody to hear it from anyone but him. It was very important to him."

The call that Gary remembers getting from Martin was to say that he was going public about his sexual abuse. Today Gary says he had no idea what exactly Martin would be saying. Martin was going to make his private experiences public, and nobody in the family thought this was a good idea. They didn't think it would be good for Martin—this was a personal matter. With so much stigma and shame attached even to knowing someone who has been sexually abused, well-meaning friends and family members often fear that they too will experience the repercussions. But Jayne knew that going public was what Martin needed to do and that there was no stopping him.

Kruze had his own worries about how other people would react, but everything that was happening felt right. He could make all the trips in the world to therapy and residential treatment centres, but nothing gave him the feeling of power like being able to name his abuser and know that he was going to be arrested.

The next morning, Thursday, February 18, Metro Toronto Police detectives Dave Tredrea and Blair Davey arrived at an apartment building on Eglinton Avenue East in Scarborough. They went to the apartment number they had been given and knocked on the door. When Gordon Stuckless answered the door, they arrested him. As they returned to the main floor to take Stuckless out to the police car, they were met by a television crew from City TV, who filmed Stuckless being led out of the building in handcuffs. The detectives would soon learn that Martin Kruze had tipped the media—he wanted Stuckless's arrest filmed and broadcast all over the city.

That same day, Martin Kruze sat at home in his basement apartment with Jayne. There, surrounded by journalists from scores of media outlets—Global TV, CBC Evening News, CBC Prime Time News, the *Globe and Mail,* the *Toronto Sun,* CTV, ON TV (now CHTV), BBS News, and others—he read from a statement he had prepared for the occasion. This one he titled his "Press Release." And so Martin Kruze went public. Unlike virtually every other victim of sexual assault, Kruze declared to the media that he wanted to be identified. They were not to disguise him in any way. He wanted everyone to know that he was the person who was publicly naming Gordon Stuckless as his abuser. He then read from his statement. The words that he had put together so carefully first for his civil suit and then for the police were now going to go across the country via the media. Kruze first named George Hannah, "a person of power, in an executive position, who would sit in Harold Ballard's box," as the man who had abused him repeatedly within the arena, from the time Kruze was thirteen until he was twenty. Kruze then named Gordon Stuckless, "an equipment maintenance worker for visiting NHL hockey teams," as another abuser. "I hope all of you survivors out there come out and make phone calls to the police," Kruze said, "and tell them about Gord Stuckless."

Through newspapers, television networks, and radio stations across the country, Kruze revealed how Hannah and Stuckless had showered him and other boys with expensive meals, equipment, and access to hockey and concert tickets. Along with the kindness and attention came individual and group acts of sexual abuse in various offices and locations in Maple Leaf Gardens. He told how the seven-plus years of abuse continued to take its toll on him long after he was able to break away from his abusers. He said that he had turned to drugs, alcohol, and sex to try to deaden the pain of his experiences. And he had made multiple suicide attempts. "I'm not doing this for money," he told the *Toronto Star*'s Dale Brazao. "I'm doing it for justice. I'm doing it so I can finally start healing."

After Kruze's accusations were widely publicized, the Gardens' management scrambled to deny responsibility. They cited the 1995 pact—what they called a "secret settlement"—for $60,000 between the Leafs organization, Kruze, and the insurance company as evidence that although the Gardens had done nothing wrong, they had acted in good faith when Kruze had complained earlier about Stuckless and the organization's knowledge of his sexual abuse. "We did everything legally that we had to do," said Brian Bellmore, speaking for Leafs owner Steve Stavro. "Maple Leaf Gardens responded promptly.... We dealt with it in what we thought was a proper way. It would have cost as much if not more to defend it as to settle it."

It was an outrageous statement, and the media were quick to pounce on it. Writing in the *Toronto Star,* columnist Rosie DiManno said that in light of Kruze's allegations of abuse at the Gardens, "it is even more appalling if the Gardens could have done something to halt any [earlier] alleged sexual misconduct.... The stink of it is nauseating."

In the *Globe and Mail,* Michael Valpy said that "stripped of all of the lawyer-crafted statements and no-comments and obfuscating blah-blah-blah, the evidence is irrefutable that officials at the great holy shrine of Canadian hockey had information that boys were possibly being sexually assaulted on its premises, and did not inform the police."

Another *Star* columnist, Dave Perkins, said that "clearly, the Maple Leafs have a duty to step forward and do the right thing here, not act as they have ... with the number of alleged victims mounting daily, this case is not going to go away."

And *Toronto Sun* sports columnist Steve Simmons, perhaps the most vocal of the media critics on how the affair was handled by the Leafs, wrote that the team "apparently chose to have it swept under the carpet. That is where they wish this story was now, lost with the dust. But instead this is a story growing legs and arms, with human victims and lives in despair.... The dirt is not about to go away. The stains around Maple Leaf Gardens are everywhere."

Martin Kruze's disclosure—and the persistent media airplay that accompanied it—had a profound effect on other men who, it would soon be revealed, had endured similar experiences. Most significantly, many of these men, who one way or another had attempted to block out memories of their abuse, were shocked to see their abusers named and pictured in the media. This was the first the survivors had seen of them in nearly two decades.

Three days later, after nonstop follow-up interviews with the press, Jayne could see that Martin was becoming exhausted. She asked the last of the media to leave. The talking that Martin had needed to do so badly was now turning into slurred and garbled words. Jayne began to worry that there was something wrong with him. He was on antidepressants and another pill to combat the side effects. He began to hallucinate. Jayne was so afraid that she called an ambulance to take him to the hospital, and then she called Gary and asked him to meet them there. Gary arrived fearing that Martin had snapped and was convinced that he should be admitted.

Martin was storming around the hospital, looking and acting as if he were crazy. It turned out that he had overdosed on the medication to combat the side effects of his antidepressants. When he had felt his mouth becoming fuzzy and weird, he took extra, thinking that that would solve the problem.

After Martin became stable, he was able to leave the hospital. The man whose actions would play such a pivotal role in the lives of hundreds of others was being taken home to bed.

NOBODY KNEW ABOUT IT

KEN COMEAU GREW UP in Regent Park in Toronto and first met Gordon Stuckless as a substitute gym teacher at Park Public School.

When I was in the shower and when I was in the dressing room drying off, he would come in and sit across from me and look at me. It was a strange feeling. He would say that I was a good kid. So when Gord's saying this to you, it made you feel all the more special. It made you feel important, it made you feel wanted.

It got to where he would start showing up at the ice rink next to our house and he would play shinny with us sometimes two, three times a week. Once in a while he would bring hockey sticks and on occasion he would give me tickets for wrestling matches or for Toronto Marlies hockey games. And for me, I thought it was another world. "Wow, hockey!" The closest I ever got to hockey was see-ing it on TV—and here I was right in the Gardens. On some occasions he would sit up in the bleach-ers with me and that was where there were some-times sexual advances. It was almost like he was testing the waters. He would put his hand on your lap sometimes and give your lap a little rub. And

*as a kid you really don't think much of it. [Then]
he would put his hand on my lap and rub my
crotch and I would be scared. It was almost like, I
feel as though it's wrong and I don't know what
I can do about it. I don't know what I should do
about it. . . . I knew from hanging around my
friends and the way they would talk: "queers" and
"fags" and everything and that's when I would get
the feeling . . . if Gord's doing that, does that mean
I'm queer? I know there's something wrong here.
That should not have happened with Gord. After
the games he would take me down closer. He
would introduce me to some of the players. You
know, I felt as though somebody was actually
paying attention to me.*

*Oh no, nobody knew about it. The only ones
who knew about it were Gord and myself. And
that's the way I wanted to keep it. . . . I was always
fearful that somebody was going to catch him
doing it and people would know it was me he was
doing it to. . . . I didn't want my mother to know
that something was going on, 'cause then I would
be punished.*

*For many years after I felt dirty. And all he can
say is, "Everything's going to be okay, kid. It's
going to be okay. Don't tell anybody." It's guys like
that your parents should warn you about.*

6

THE INVESTIGATION

The pain that these guys were in was phenomenal.
The majority broke down in tears every time we spoke
to them—it was very very difficult for each and every
one of them.
　　—Detective Dave Tredrea, 2001

THE INVESTIGATION WENT FROM extraordinary to mind-boggling in no time at all. The police initially laid two charges of gross indecency and indecent assault against Gordon Stuckless for what he had done to Martin Kruze. Stuckless was now sitting in jail awaiting a bail hearing.

The media coverage of Stuckless's arrest was fierce. "Gardens left scrambling over scandal," screamed the headline in one Toronto daily, while others blared news of a "Sex Ring" and a "Pedophile Ring" in operation at the Gardens in the 1970s, where "sex orgies" abounded. But despite all of the sensationalism, Detective Dave Tredrea says today that this was one case in which the media always seemed to be a step ahead of the police. He credited Kruze with some of the tip-offs. He also believed that some of the people who had information to report felt more comfortable contacting the media first—they could get information off their chests without worrying about becoming part of an official record, and the media steered the callers to the police anyway. Tredrea says that he and his partner, Blair Davey, were reading about John Paul Roby as an alleged suspect before anyone had made an official report to the police about him. Martin Kruze had named him in his letter as someone he strongly suspected of abusing boys because of what he had seen at Maple Leaf Gardens and because Roby had tried to get close to him.

The calls started pouring into 52 Division. Seventy to eighty people called each day to report information to the police about the two men Kruze had already accused, two men that he hadn't, and just about everything else that went on at Maple Leaf Gardens over a thirty-year period. If someone's bicycle had been stolen, the police heard about it. They heard from men who said they had been victimized as Martin Kruze had, and they heard from others who said that Stuckless and Hannah had tried but not succeeded in abusing them. The men in this group reported that Stuckless and Hannah had done things that made them feel weird or uncomfortable and that they had told their parents, who warned them to stay away from the men. The parents' actions protected their own children, but many hadn't seemed to consider that if their children were being approached, other boys could be targets as well.

Back then, some of the parents did worry. They wrote letters to Maple Leaf Gardens warning that Gordon Stuckless was a child abuser. Barry Bingham was one of those parents. Not only had Stuckless tried to abuse his son, he had succeeded. When Stuckless sexually assaulted Bingham's son Darryl in 1987, Darryl told his parents after it had happened several times. His parents had taught him that no one should ever touch his private parts. It was because of this instruction that Darryl knew he had to tell them. Finally he did, and even though Stuckless coached minor hockey with Bingham and was considered a friend of the family, Bingham called the police. Stuckless was charged, pleaded guilty, and was sentenced to thirty or sixty days—Bingham can't remember which, but he does remember being told at the time that this was a good sentence. The whole court process took longer than the amount of time that Stuckless served. It did create a legal record, however: Stuckless would be on record for having sexually assaulted a boy in 1987.

Bingham and his wife alerted all of the families who had been involved in hockey and agreed to be interviewed anonymously for an article published in the *Toronto Star* by Lois Kalchman on June 11, 1988, warning about the risks of abuse in minor hockey. Bingham also sent a letter to Donald Giffen, a Maple Leaf Gardens official, telling him that Leafs employee Gordon Stuckless had sexually assaulted his son. Bingham knew how much it meant to Stuckless to work there and to take boys there for games and tours, and he knew that Stuckless looked after the Leafs' kids. Bingham wanted Maple Leaf Gardens to

know they had a sex offender working for them. He received a
letter back two weeks later thanking him for his concern and
advising that they were aware of the problem. Although Martin
Kruze's abuse was long over by 1987, during that year he tried
to take his own life for the first time. It is unsettling to think
that Gordon Stuckless was sexually abusing another child
around the same time that Martin was suffering the effects of his
abuse so acutely.

The police met with Maple Leaf Gardens management early
in the investigation and found them to be completely cooperative. They would do whatever they could to help. Given the
size of the organization, and the number of full- and part-time
employees, Tredrea thought that the best way to get information would be to develop a questionnaire for management to
pass on to staff. He wanted only those with information rele-
vant to the investigation to complete the form and submit it.
"We were not contacted by one person who worked at Maple
Leaf Gardens. Nobody had any damning evidence," said Tredrea.
"It was quickly apparent that the employees there definitely
had the feeling of being part of a family. There was definitely
a sense of belonging there, and nobody was going to betray
the Gardens."

The police did, however, hear from a Gardens employee.
The media had received calls saying that John Paul Roby, who
still worked there as a part-time usher, had abused boys at
Maple Leaf Gardens, and several newspaper and TV reporters
had gone to his home to try to interview him. Roby called the

police to complain that the media were bothering him. Tredrea and Davey had been trying to arrest him earlier that day, so Tredrea gave him a choice: "Turn yourself in or we'll come and get you." According to press reports at the time, Roby picked up his paycheque from Maple Leaf Gardens and then took the streetcar over to 52 Division to turn himself in. Roby was arrested and held in jail awaiting a bail hearing.

The police wanted to meet anyone living in the Toronto area who identified himself or herself as a victim. Because they wanted to follow up the initial contacts with formal, videotaped interviews, they asked victims who lived in other parts of the province or the country to make reports to their local police stations. Tredrea and Davey handled all of the Toronto area calls. They expected that they might hear from some of the people Kruze had listed in his material whom they hadn't been able to locate before, and they also expected there would be some others Kruze had not listed. Within only a few days, the numbers became overwhelming. By the end of the first week, sixty men had called identifying themselves as victims of George Hannah, John Paul Roby, and/or Gordon Stuckless.

The media coverage of the arrests of Stuckless and Roby had a devastating effect on many of the men who'd suffered abuse at their hands. Most of the men learned about the arrests on TV or through the newspapers, and seeing Stuckless's and Roby's faces again brought horrible memories flooding back. But as unpleasant as these memories were, Martin Kruze hoped they would be the catalyst for getting survivors of abuse like him to take the giant step of coming forward and telling the police of their own experiences. As painful as it was for all of them—and by the end of the first couple of months of the investigation, nearly one hundred survivors would come forward—it was worth it for the greater good Kruze hoped to accomplish. The case against Gordon Stuckless was getting stronger and stronger with each new accusation.

Steve Sutton remembers the day he called the police after seeing Gordon Stuckless's picture on TV. "I heard his name, and I looked up and there was his face," he says. As Sutton listened to the police appealing for other victims to come forward, he thought back to his own abuse. He thought about what Stuckless had done to him and wondered how he could possibly go about explaining it to the police. What had happened was always there. He had vowed he would never tell a soul about it. Now he wanted to help but didn't want to tell.

Soon Sutton's urge to come forward overwhelmed his vow to stay silent. The police were asking for help, and he could help them. He decided to head down to the police station the following day. He told his wife that he had to go out to the police station. "Here, watch this newscast," he said. "I'm a victim of that." His wife said, "What?" He repeated what he had said and then told her that it had happened when he was eight or nine. Gordon Stuckless had been his lacrosse coach, and he had never told anyone. He wanted his wife to know where he was going, but he still didn't want to tell her anything about it. Sutton, like many victims, had locked his abuse away, determined that he would never tell because of the shame. He hid his abuse from everyone, including his mother, his brothers and sisters, and later his wife and children. As a teenager, Sutton began smoking dope and became addicted to it for the next twenty years.

Unlike Kruze, who had spent months preparing to go to the police and had his partner, Jayne Dunsmore, to accompany him, Sutton made his decision in one day and went alone. Although he was "very, very nervous," he didn't want company, because he still really didn't want anyone to know what had happened to him. He circled the block before he decided to go through with it.

Sutton had expected that he would tell the police what had happened and that that would be the end of the interview. But the police had many questions they wanted him to answer. Who were his teachers? Where had he met Stuckless? What had Stuckless given him? Sutton was taken aback; he had only been thinking about telling them about the abuse that he still pictured so clearly in his mind. He figures now that they were checking out his credibility. Was he really clear about what had happened? Did the pieces fit together? He smiled when he thought about telling them that he couldn't remember the name of his first-grade teacher because he hadn't been paying much attention in school that year.

Sutton told the police that Gordon Stuckless had been his coach in lacrosse and that he had sexually abused him when he played in the Beaches Box Lacrosse League, where he and his family spent a lot of time. Stuckless would detain him in the change room so that he would be the last one there. He also abused Steve in the bathroom of the Sutton house. Stuckless frequently needed a place to stay and always seemed available to help out. He offered to babysit Steve and his brothers and sisters in exchange for accommodation. Sutton's mother welcomed Stuckless's help, since he seemed to be a kind and friendly man. He played lacrosse and hockey with all of the kids right out on the street in front of their house.

Even though the police interview was taxing, Sutton was relieved to finally get the words out: "I felt great afterwards that I was able to get it off my chest and maybe help them in whatever way I could."

Another victim, Derrick Brown (called Ricky as a boy), caught the news and immediately called his sister and asked what she thought he should do. She told him to pick up the phone and call the police. He called the police, and just saying the words on the phone opened up his memories about what had happened to him and his twenty years of living with it. Even though his sister had been very supportive when he told her about his abuse a few years earlier, he worried about how the police would respond.

When the police interviewed Brown, he said that Gordon Stuckless had been his hockey coach and had taken him to games at Maple Leaf Gardens and given him tours of the building. Stuckless asked Derrick if he would like to help him fix his roof, and Derrick was proud to be asked. Stuckless said that he would treat him to dinner and a game at the Gardens; the next day they would get to work on the roof. Derrick's parents knew how much Derrick liked his coach and agreed to let him spend the evening and sleep over at Stuckless's. During the night he woke to find that Stuckless "was doing something he shouldn't have been doing." Terrified, Derrick jumped out of bed and went to stay on the couch in the living room. He couldn't think to do anything else. He lay there frozen, frightened that something else would happen. The next morning Stuckless told him not to worry, that he did this with other boys. Derrick went home as soon as he could and put it completely out of his mind.

Brown told the police that when Stuckless and he visited at Maple Leaf Gardens, Stuckless had been friendly there in a "touchy" kind of way, but nothing had prepared him for what happened when he went over to help Stuckless fix his roof. Stuckless had used Maple Leaf Gardens to build his relationship with Derrick Brown, though the physical assault itself did not take place there.

When Brian Silber heard the news he phoned his probation officer. She became the first person he ever told. He told her that what had happened to Martin Kruze had happened to him too. "I cried and I told her all about it," Silber said. "I was more embarrassed at first, but she listened to me." Silber had tried to tell his mother when he was younger, but he could never open his mouth to say the words. Now Silber was telling his probation officer that he had been abused by Gordon Stuckless, George Hannah, and John Paul Roby at Maple Leaf Gardens. Silber agreed to speak to the police, and they met and interviewed him at the probation office. Silber wanted the police to know what the three men had done to him and he also wanted them to know something else. He told the police that once Stuckless sexually abused him in Harold Ballard's office, in front of Ballard. Silber wanted everyone to know that as far as he was concerned there would be no justice for him, because no matter what could still be done to Stuckless and Roby, Ballard would never be held accountable for what he let go on directly in front of him.

Ken Comeau was interviewed by the police in his hometown of Paris, Ontario. The interview was a turning point for him. It was the first time he had ever had a positive experience with the police, and to this day the officer who interviewed him always waves to say hello. Comeau laughs, "Cops aren't as bad as we think they are."

The interview was tough. As difficult as it had been for Comeau to tell his wife after he broke down reading about Stuckless's arrest in the newspaper at work, telling the most intimate details of his life to a stranger was even harder. In his videotaped interview, Comeau reported that Stuckless befriended him, his brothers, his mother, and his stepfather. Stuckless always turned up at just the right time and took Ken for drives in his car, out to the drive-in movie theatre, and down to Maple Leaf Gardens. He even taught Ken to drive. When Ken's hands were fixed on the steering wheel, Stuckless would lean over and reach into his pants and touch his penis. If Stuckless was visiting at the Comeaus' house and it got too late, he would stay over, and then he would slip into Ken's room, most often to say good night. Once Ken woke up in horror: Stuckless had his mouth on Ken's penis. To this day, Comeau pictures the assault vividly.

Comeau reported to the police that Stuckless gave him things like a hockey stick with a red fiberglass blade and other equipment. He also told the police that whenever Stuckless took him to the Gardens they sat way up high in the grey seats and didn't move down until later in the practice. Stuckless abused him in the grey section, where nobody else was ever around. Ken Comeau never understood why they didn't sit down closer to the ice where everybody else sat.

Clifford Wright was also interviewed by police in his hometown of Orangeville, Ontario. He still lived in the same part of town where he had grown up. When he saw the report that Gordon Stuckless had been charged with abusing Martin Kruze at Maple Leaf Gardens, he said: "Holy mackerel, it happened to somebody else." But Wright had never met Gordon Stuckless; it was John Paul Roby who had abused him. When he called the police in Toronto they told him to contact his local police department. Wright felt immediately that they weren't that interested in what he wanted to tell them. He did follow up with Orangeville police, but it would have been easy for him not to. In his videotaped statement, Wright told the police that he was abused by John Paul Roby in 1969.

By March 4, the police had received reports from eighty-one men. Many of the men reported that they had known their

abusers through several different means. While many were
abused at Maple Leaf Gardens, many were not. The men who
had not been abused at Maple Leaf Gardens said that Stuckless
had abused them in their homes, in his home, in his car, at the
drive-in movie theatre, in the dressing room at school, during
gym class at school, in his office at school, in the change room at
the local rink, on the ice, and so on. He had given some of them
things like hockey sticks and player autographs, but others had
been given nothing. He took some to dinner but not others. He
made friends with the families of some of the boys but not with
others. Every time the police briefed the media they stated that
Gordon Stuckless had been active all over and outside of the
city, and yet the media consistently focused on the "sex scandal"
at Maple Leaf Gardens, "where boys were lured with promises of
hockey futures, tickets and more," where the boys received
"privileges and favours in exchange for sex."

A number of factors came together to fuel this situation.
Kruze's own very public description of what had happened to
him and the constant telling and retelling of that story in-
fluenced the subsequent reports. Kruze himself used terms and
phrases like "sex ring" and "group sex" and "lured with tickets
and autographs," and his focus was on—above anything else—
the fact that the abuse had occurred at Maple Leaf Gardens over
a long period of time and in many different locations on the
premises. When the other men came forward, none of whom
were planning to tell about their abuse in quite the way it ended
up happening—if ever at all—they told the police what hap-

pened to them. The police briefed the media, and they continued to blend the new reports into the existing story. The information that boys had been given passes and hockey equipment was told and retold in the media until it became reduced to "sex in exchange for privileges." But Gordon Stuckless didn't have to lure any boys to Maple Leaf Gardens—they wanted to go. He didn't give them things in order to have sex with them—he gave them gifts as part of the "friendship" he developed with them because he knew how much it meant to them. He didn't say, "I'll do this for you if I can suck on your penis"; he did all kinds of things for the boys, as an attentive and generous adult might do, and then he attacked them.

Further, many of the men had little understanding of the dynamics of their abuse when they came forward, because they had tried to shove every detail about the abuse as far away from themselves as possible. In interviews Brian Silber wondered why he would have allowed himself to go back to Maple Leaf Gardens over and over again. It turned out that since he was only nine at the time, it hadn't been his decision at all. Gordon Stuckless had taken him there. Silber believed so strongly that he had been responsible for "letting" Stuckless abuse him that he didn't even realize that if the older man had not been transporting him there, he never would have ended up in the building. Stuckless also drove him to his hockey games because Brian was the goalie and had so much equipment to carry.

When Brian Silber's team made the playoffs at Maple Leaf Gardens and he played the most important game of his minor hockey league life, he couldn't even enjoy the victory because he knew that Stuckless would be waiting for him in the dressing room, that he would abuse him and then take him home. That's a radically different picture from the one most often presented in the media coverage of the "Gardens Sex Scandal," with boys being admitted to the Gardens in exchange for sex.

On March 4, 1997, Martin Kruze and many of the men who had made allegations against Gordon Stuckless sat in court for Stuckless's bail hearing. It was held over for yet another week because of all the new charges. Many of the men came up to Kruze and introduced themselves to him. They thanked him for having the courage to be the first to come forward. Each had believed that he was the only one that this had happened to— now there seemed to be so many of them. They wondered who else was still out there.

A publication ban was imposed to protect the victims' identities. Kruze stated explicitly that he wanted to be excluded from the ban; he wanted to continue speaking freely to the press. That day, Kruze was reported to say about Stuckless: "He's gutless and he couldn't look me in the eye. I'll be here until he does." Although many of the men were too embarrassed and ashamed to do anything more than just quietly thank him, they respected him for doing what many had pledged to themselves they never would do.

Rosie DiManno wrote the next day that Kruze was sitting on the bench outside the court and heard, as did many others, one of the female reporters comment that she was tiring of the

Gardens story and was looking forward to moving on to something else. DiManno noted that the media had gobbled up the story to begin with and had been generally sympathetic to Kruze and the scores of other victims coming forward. Now she was hearing other comments: Why would an abused boy keep returning to his abuser? Why didn't the boys stop it sooner? What about fraudulent claims? DiManno suggested that such questions showed a complete lack of understanding of the dynamics of child sexual abuse and an underlying belief that children are somehow responsible for the behaviour of adults. In response to the idea that people might falsely represent themselves as victims of abuse, DiManno wrote: "The suggestion that, somehow, huge numbers of people willingly would put themselves through the process of formally complaining to police, testifying in court, subjecting themselves to the rigors of cross-examination, is ridiculous. A sick soul or two might try it, I suppose, but not many."

By March 12 the number of complainants against Stuckless had risen to thirty-three. Roby was charged with thirty-five counts of indecent assault, thirty-one counts of gross indecency, two counts of buggery, and two counts of initiating sexual touching for a total of seventy charges involving fifty-one people.

The police met a second time with Leafs general manager and president Cliff Fletcher to update him on the progress of the case. He pledged his continued cooperation and announced that an internal investigation would be conducted at Maple Leaf Gardens as well. According to the *Globe and Mail,* when

members of the press asked Fletcher and Leafs representative
Brian Bellmore about how Gardens management had handled
Kruze's complaint and subsequent suit lodged in 1993, Fletcher
stated that they had turned it over to their insurance company
to handle. Royal Insurance investigated the claims and wasn't
even sure if there was any validity to the complaint. The company said that there was no evidence that other boys were
involved. At worst it was an isolated incident, if it were even a
legitimate incident at that. Gardens management accepted the
findings of the report and "the lawyers for both sides made a
business deal." The *Globe* further quoted Detective Tredrea as
saying that legally, the Gardens had not been required to report
Kruze's allegations to the police after he had informed Maple
Leaf Gardens management of them, "but morally, maybe they
should have."

The current Gardens employees may not have wanted to say
anything, but former employees and men who had played on
teams that held practices and games at the Gardens during the
1970s and 1980s contacted the media and police to say that had
the investigator contacted any of them, he would have been told
that the abuse was common knowledge. One man interviewed
by the *Globe and Mail* said he believed that he and his teammates
had been spared because they had free passes to the Gardens
and could go anywhere they wanted. They wouldn't have
needed to be "enticed." He believed that it was the boys who
didn't have the same degree of access who would have been
subjected to the assaults. Some of the former employees said

there were always rumours floating around about certain employees. Others called to say that they had never seen or suspected a thing. Writing in 1999, author Paul Quarrington
pointed out that "it's ironic . . . to realize that this is a perverted
aspect of Ballard's quirky, erratic philanthropy: he liked to give
lonely men a place to be, not realizing that their loneliness
often resulted from psychopathy."

On March 14, Martin Kruze returned to Maple Leaf Gardens
to show Detective Dave Tredrea and Walter Tyrrell, the retired
Metro police officer hired by the Gardens to review the rink's
security, exactly where he had been abused, revisiting those
areas he had photographed three years earlier. A police video-
grapher recorded the whole visit. "It was a very traumatic experience, very painful just to be in there," Kruze told the *Toronto
Star*. One of the ushers glared at him; it was as if Kruze were the
troublemaker returning to make more trouble. As cooperative
as management may have been, some employees at the Gardens
were less generous. Instead of seeing Kruze as a victim of crime,
they saw him as the one who had destroyed the good name of
Maple Leaf Gardens.

The weight of the case went beyond the number of testi-
monies that the police had to commit to videotape. Tredrea and
Davey carried the emotional and psychological weight of the
investigation on their shoulders as well. "We became the lifeline
for more than a hundred males," Tredrea recalls. "And it was
just devastating, because there was such a degree of trust that
developed between the victims and us. We were the first people

that many of them had revealed this to, and this was a secret they had kept inside for twenty-five years."

Not only were they dealing with the facts of the cases as they were developing against Stuckless and Roby, they were dealing with the men whose lives had been turned upside-down or to disaster. "When this comes to the surface, it opens up all the wounds again," Tredrea said. They quickly put victim support services into place and even began looking for counselling and support for the men. Still, they were often the ones to get the calls when any of the men were feeling scared or desperate about having opened themselves up. Tredrea recalls one time in particular. The Emergency Task Force contacted him one night when he had guests over for dinner to tell him that one of the victims had barricaded himself and was going to commit suicide. Tredrea spent the next two hours talking him out of his situation. That was just one of the many extreme circumstances that the police were called in to deal with. Other victims became depressed and suicidal but did not reach out to the police for help. Steve Sutton tried to stab himself and later another victim, Derek Goodyear, climbed on top of a bridge railing, but these acts of desperation didn't come to official attention.

After his arrest, Stuckless was denied bail. Justice Jeff Casey ordered him to be held in custody until his trial. Stuckless would remain there, undergoing psychiatric evaluation and police questioning, a full eight months, while Tredrea and Davey continued the investigation and Crown attorneys Jim Hughes and Susan Orlando—both of whom declined to be interviewed for this book, citing the ongoing nature of the case—compiled evidence against Stuckless. Officially, Stuckless faced fifty-seven counts, including gross indecency, buggery, and sexual assault against thirty-five victims.

Throughout all of this, the victims' lives hinged on every detail reported in the press. The men faced doubts and questions from their wives, girlfriends, partners, other family members, and friends and waited for every court date that was set and then reset. The men prepared themselves psychologically that soon they would have to testify in court about what Stuckless had done to them. It was one thing for them to get through the interviews with the police; it was another altogether to speak about it in a courtroom in front of other people.

Many of the men had experienced the classic after-effects of abuse—addiction, depression, problems with employment, damaged personal relationships—and were worried that their pasts would be brought up in court as a way of discrediting them. Even though Martin Kruze had such a history, he was not worried; he was as determined as ever to speak about what Gordon Stuckless had done and what it had cost him. Even though his abuser was in custody, Kruze had a long way to go before he could feel vindicated. He needed to let as many people as possible know what he'd been through. By speaking out, he was also seeing how much he could help other survivors. And that was the next task he set for himself.

The Pain Doesn't Go Away

LIKE MARTIN KRUZE, other survivors of sexual abuse by Hannah, Stuckless, or Roby remained in despair long after their abuse ended.

> *I can't go past Church Street and that without having those bad things come out of the doors and out of the walls. It's terrible; I can't even walk by there.* —Brian Silber

> *Even when my daughter was growing up I hardly ever tucked her in, or hugged her, or kissed her for fear someone might accuse me of abusing her. I know it has affected her. I never allowed myself to get too close.* —Clifford Wright

> *You go through the first seven or eight years of your marriage believing that you love someone but not understanding why or how they could ever love you. Ever. They must want something. They must want to take advantage of something, somehow. And to be perfectly honest, I don't know if I could tell you sitting right here today what love really is. What being in love is. Boy I wish I could. Because love is what's around me and yet that same love is still something that frightens me. And*

*that all ties back to having someone take away my
ability to trust with all my heart.* —Thomas Allan

*A lot of people don't understand it. They think
you'll get over it. You don't. You don't get over it.
It's been over half my life and I still can't get over
it. When you're lying in bed at night and you're
trying to get a half-decent sleep—no, you can't.
You have a fear of going to sleep.* —Ken Comeau

I've lost my family over this, my children, my wife.
—Brian Silber

7

MARTIN'S CRUSADE

For most people, if they can get it right, in their own
private world in some way, shape or form, then they've
done an heroic job and it really isn't necessary to do
the other.
  —Sylvia Fraser, 1999

IN THE MONTHS FOLLOWING his dramatic public disclosure of
sexual abuse, Martin Kruze became Canada's poster boy for the
cause. Sylvia Fraser was its poster girl in the late 1980s and
early 1990s. "The other" she refers to above is what she, Kruze,
and so many other victims of sexual abuse at one time or
another find themselves compelled to do. Having lived with
such isolation and shame, they make their abuse public in the
hope that the costs to them personally will not have been in
vain and that others may be spared their experiences.

Fraser lived this "other," public life following the 1987 release
of the book *My Father's House,* about her own experiences of

sexual abuse by her father. Martin Kruze was living that public life now. And true to form, Kruze put into it everything he had.

Kruze transformed himself into a professional survivor of sexual abuse. He created a business card, letterhead, and fax cover sheets adorned with the popular yellow happy face, and the word "survivor" was proudly displayed across the top of his stationery. He prepared packages containing extensive material related to his abuse for the journalists and writers who requested interviews with him, and he followed up every interview on radio or TV with a letter of thanks and an offer to return at a future date. Kruze was as professional in these undertakings as he had been in any of his other business dealings. He always wore a suit and elegant black leather shoes with tassels to his media interviews. In contrast to his days with Diana Roman, when he looked "nerdy," Kruze couldn't have looked better put-together. No detail was overlooked—Kruze knew how to sell, and he knew how to sell himself and his cause. It was as if his life depended on it.

Throughout the time that the Stuckless case was being prepared for prosecution, Kruze continued his courtship with the media. His goal was to raise awareness about sexual abuse and offer support to other survivors. He freely identified himself as a survivor of abuse, although until his offender was convicted, Kruze was technically not a victim of any crime. However, Kruze had lived the abuse and defined himself as a survivor— how the matter was handled by the court system was always a secondary concern for him. This approach had other repercussions for Kruze. Talk show interviews, for example, identified him as the person who had accused Stuckless (and Hannah) of abusing him, rather than as the person who was victimized by them or had survived abuse by them.

Kruze made the rounds on daytime television and radio talk shows: *Canada AM* with Valerie Pringle, *The Dini Petty Show*, and *Jane Hawtin Live* were just a few. This last program was a popular TV talk show that featured a phone-in component, in which viewers could air their thoughts about the day's topic. Hawtin also broadcast on radio, Talk 640.

Hawtin was committed to covering the Gardens case. She had interviewed Sheldon Kennedy when he came forward, and long before that she had interviewed some of the men who had been abused at the St. John's Training School when she had been on CFRB radio. Hawtin remembered the transformation that Kruze made from his first interview with her on Talk 640 radio to his first appearance on her television show. "I had never quite seen that—someone so quickly understand how the media works, how you have to speak, how you have to present yourself," says Hawtin. She had interviewed many people who had been victimized by some act or tragedy and then later become advocates for others—that was the role she saw Kruze taking on. She likens Kruze's and Kennedy's efforts: "Because they know about the secrecy that has to be involved with something like sexual abuse, they know that pulling back the veil, as hard as it is to do, is so important. And I think it's a real privilege when you get to be a part of that, especially when you hear those voices from all over the country."

Kruze appeared on *Jane Hawtin Live* along with an expert on sex offenders and Gordon Kirke, a lawyer well known in the sports community and the agent for high-profile NHL star Eric Lindros. At the time, Kirke was working on a report about harassment and abuse for the Canadian Hockey League. The impetus and inspiration for the report had been Sheldon Kennedy.

Kruze answered Hawtin's questions calmly, reiterating how Hannah and Stuckless had set him up and abused him, and emphasizing his belief that he'd make it through the aftermath of the case "with God's help." All the callers who phoned in expressed their support for what he'd done in bringing the abuse at Maple Leaf Gardens to public attention. "Now you know you are not alone," one caller said. Several of them became extremely emotional as they related their own experiences of abuse. Steadfastly, Kruze told them that he supported them, that they needed to get a therapist who was an expert on abuse, and that he'd be saying a prayer for them. One caller broke down and told Kruze that he was his hero for having taken the first step forward. Kruze responded that it was the caller who was the hero now for having the courage to call in to the show and get support for himself.

When Martin returned home after the show, many messages were waiting for him, but the two that meant the most came from his mother and his brother Gary. Martin wrote

them down word for word. Gary told him how classy he had
been and what a good thing he had done. He said that he
respected him and knew that others would too because there
was a lot of compassion for what had happened to him. His
mother couldn't say enough times how proud she was of him.
He had already helped so many by coming forward and now
he was helping even more. "I am very proud of you, very
proud, because you are fighting the worst silent killer in the
country, abuse," she said.

Rex Murphy of CBC *Newsmagazine* would later observe that
Kruze "rocketed from secrecy and anonymity to the mock fame
of talk show guest—that wedding of confession, entertainment
and pseudo-therapy and intimacy." Kruze did take on the role
of counsellor and mentor to the show's callers. It felt good to be
helping others, and he knew how important it was to be
acknowledged. He was offering callers affirmation of their
experiences from someone who could truly say he understood
their pain. As much as Murphy seemed to dismiss this function,
Kruze was performing a public service, and viewers and listen-
ers lapped it up. But it was nevertheless true that in a very short
time Martin Kruze had gone from a confused, lonely man to a
public figure—one whose darkest secrets were now a matter of
public record.

Following the show, Kruze persisted with his offers to help
Gordon Kirke. Not only did he offer to provide Kirke with any
other information that could be helpful to his research, but
he also reminded Kirke that he could be a support to other

survivors whom Kirke might interview. It was clear to Kirke that Kruze was on a mission and that he had endless energy to devote to his cause.

Kruze sent his ideas and suggestions to Kirke by fax. Kirke says, "I can remember days that were the darkest for me when I really thought, my God, what have I gotten myself into—and just feeling very mired in it and seeing a very sad side of society. And I'd get a fax sheet coming from Martin with this happy face, and it never failed to brighten up what I was doing. . . . His timing was uncanny—it would arrive at the time I needed it most."

Through his work on the report, Kirke learned a lot about sexual abuse that relates to thousands of others like Martin Kruze. When he began the report, he believed, as did many others, that sexual abuse happened to girls. When his daughter and son went to camp, he would warn his daughter about inappropriate touching from others, but all he would say to his son was, "Now don't you drown."

He also discovered that anyone who saw him reading a book with any mention of sexual abuse in the title avoided contact with him. Parents even steered their children away from him if they got too close. Kirke began to realize that if this was how he was being treated, survivors must often be regarded with suspicion and fear rather than being given the belief and support they needed.

Kirke also met people who questioned Kruze's motives. They wondered why he was so keen to help and suggested that he was a "guy just trying to put the squeeze on the Gardens."

Kirke heard other questions and comments about survivors of sexual abuse: Why are they saying this now? Why didn't they stop it sooner? They must have liked what was going on. They must be homosexual. And so on. The more Kirke met and talked to people like Kruze and the more he heard cynical comments from others, the more he realized that "one of the roughest things that survivors are up against is the cynicism they face in society. And that caused me a lot of anger." Kruze himself seemed to realize that abuse is such an affront that people strike out at the person bringing it to light.

Kirke credits Martin Kruze with enlightening him about such aspects of sexual abuse. When his report, called "Players First Report," was released in August 1997, Kirke formally dedicated it to Sheldon Kennedy but acknowledges Kruze's pivotal role: "the second most important was Martin, because he had stayed so in touch and had bolstered me so much throughout." Kruze, along with Kennedy and hundreds of others, called to congratulate Kirke when the report was released.

Around this time, a lawyer approached Kruze about teaming up with a journalist to write a book about his life. One of the titles Kruze considered was *The Harold Ballard Days Sex Scandal at Toronto's Maple Leaf Gardens*. But the book would have to wait until Stuckless was convicted; Kruze was still an alleged victim of sexual abuse.

Kruze wanted to get more deeply involved in helping victims deal with sexual abuse, and people told him to call the Central Agencies Sexual Abuse Treatment Program (CASAT).

When he arrived at CASAT inquiring about volunteer opportunities, the staff were impressed by his devotion to the cause and his professional style. They were delighted to have the interest and support of someone who had so much to offer.

They also had a project they believed was ideal for Kruze. Georgia Colton and social worker Michelle Grossman had just finished writing a handbook to help youth and their parents deal with sexual abuse. Colton's own daughter had been sexually abused a few years earlier, and Colton knew what it was like to feel sick and overwhelmed and to try to get help for one's child. Colton herself had been physically abused by her father when she was a child and later by her husband. As she got to know Martin, she felt that they were kindred spirits. The CASAT team asked Kruze to be the spokesperson for the handbook. This would involve speaking at the media launch and giving interviews to the media about the handbook's value. Kruze couldn't wait to get started.

Kruze also heard about a safe house that was going to be established in the Etobicoke area to help survivors of abuse. Art Lockhart, a professor who taught criminal justice at Humber College and an abuse survivor himself, was gathering people together to resuscitate an old building that had been the gatehouse to the grounds of a former psychiatric hospital. The windows were boarded up and the door was sealed, but Lockhart believed that the building could be refurbished and become a safe place for survivors of abuse of all ages. Lockhart knew such a house was needed because over the years far too many students had come to him to tell him of their own abuse experiences. They needed a safe place to talk to someone they trusted.

Part of the reason his students turned to him was because he identified himself as a survivor of sexual abuse. Lockhart frequently found himself sitting with a student, drinking coffee, talking about what had happened to the student, and looking over at this boarded-up building. If the community could become involved, Lockhart believed, the Gatehouse could become a visible, recognizable place for abuse survivors to get help. Lockhart was convinced that if such a place had existed when he was a kid, he would have been able to get help much sooner. Kruze also believed that the Gatehouse could help. He attended the early meetings and planned to sit on its first board of directors. Kruze and Art Lockhart also became fast friends—they met for coffee and talked as two survivors about things that men rarely talk about: sexual abuse and the difficulty of trying to get the word out.

When the handbook was published and CASAT tried to proceed with its plans to hold the media launch at police headquarters, police officials decided that if Kruze was participating, the launch could not be held there. They supported the handbook, but their officials argued that allowing Kruze to be present would be the equivalent of presuming that Stuckless was guilty before he was tried. CASAT had to make a hard choice: drop Kruze as the spokesperson or find a new location for the launch. CASAT moved the launch to the YMCA, where there was strong support for helping individuals speak out about their experiences.

One of the people who attended the launch was Michael Irving—an artist, psychotherapist, and survivor of abuse. He was building a monument to serve as a permanent, public testament to those who had survived sexual abuse. To be titled "Reaching Out," the monument would be composed of two large graceful bronze figures standing together in a protective arc of hopeful, outstretched arms. Each figure would be cloaked in a bronze tapestry of quilt squares, each of which would contain the handprint of a survivor of sexual abuse (or a supporter of the cause) and a message created by that individual. When Kruze met Irving that day, he told him that he would like to come to the studio to cast his handprint and make a square to go on the monument.

After the launch Kruze began to develop a plan to get more money to produce more copies of the handbook for CASAT. He wanted one available to every child in the city, and he wanted it translated into other languages as well. He had collected a whole binder's worth of business cards, and he wrote out a long list of names and addresses that he would write to on CASAT's behalf. He included his personal and business contacts as well as the many companies that did business with the Toronto Maple Leafs. He even sent a letter to Steve Stavro asking Maple Leaf Gardens to donate money to help produce more handbooks. He loved taking shots at the Gardens. Maybe this time they would act on his request and do something to help survivors of child abuse. Unfortunately, not one of Martin's letters produced money to reprint the handbook. Those contacts that responded said that their charitable contributions had already been decided for that year. Maple Leaf Gardens never even replied.

Between CASAT, the Gatehouse, and public appearances, Kruze was a busy man. He also conceived of the idea of hosting a television show devoted exclusively to sexual abuse issues. Kruze spent hours making telephone calls and sending out faxes with ideas for show topics to the various journalists he had met.

Kruze was thrilled when he was asked to appear on *Oprah*. But it turned out to be the next time that his status as an "alleged victim" reared its head. He and Sheldon Kennedy were to be the guests, and eager to appear on the show, Martin agreed to make the trip to Chicago even though they wouldn't pay for Jayne to accompany him as his support.

It wasn't until he arrived in Chicago—filled with excitement about having an opportunity to raise millions of people's awareness about child sexual abuse all in one shot—that he discovered that he and Jayne were not staying in the same hotel as Kennedy and his wife. And even though Kruze had expressly stated his desire to meet and talk with Kennedy before or after the show, Kruze was not given access to him. Finally, when it was time for the show to begin, Martin and Jayne were led to front-row seats in the audience, while Sheldon Kennedy and his wife took their places on stage, next to Oprah Winfrey. Winfrey interviewed Kennedy from his chair as "guest" and then interviewed Kruze from his front row seat as "audience member."

Kruze had never understood that he was not going to be a guest on stage along with Kennedy. Further, Winfrey seemed uncomfortable with Kruze's interview in particular. Of all people—given her own experiences of sexual abuse as a child and her own efforts to protect children through legislation—Winfrey should have been open to what both Kennedy and Kruze had to say. But she barely even asked Kruze questions and then interrupted one of his answers by asking if he'd been abused right out in the open at Maple Leaf Gardens or in the "stadium's bleachers." Her question revealed a complete lack of sensitivity to Kruze. Further, she did not know—or had not bothered to find out—enough about hockey to use the right terms. The game is played in an arena, and the seating is commonly referred to as the "stands" or the "seats." Kruze fumbled to respond and said that he believed God was using him as an instrument to help others.

The message that Kruze gave to his friends at CASAT upon his return was that he had had a wonderful experience and that it had meant everything to him to have appeared on Oprah's show. What Kruze may have been feeling deeper down he didn't let on to anyone. Kruze maintained his public posture at all times. He worked hard for the cause, and even though he was often asked to reveal very embarrassing and intimate details about what he had experienced and how he had been affected—and he did so willingly—he never let on if things weren't going well. Occasionally Kruze would withdraw for several days at a time, and this would only be noticeable because there wouldn't be phone calls or faxes from him. One time he had to cancel a trip to Calgary for a television interview with WTN (Women's Television Network) because he wasn't feeling well. The only reason anyone other than Jayne found out about that was because the show's producers contacted CASAT looking for someone to replace him. Another time one of the CASAT staff drove by his apartment building and saw him sitting in the back of an ambulance parked in front of the building. Surprised, she called him later and suggested that he must have had some kind of accident; was he all right?

Martin Kruze was not all right; in this case, he had overdosed on prescription pills. When he couldn't go to Calgary, it was because he was too depressed to get out of bed. When he didn't return his phone calls as promptly as usual, it was because he had gone off and disappeared for several days. Even Jayne didn't know where he was when that happened, but she suspected he was somewhere doing drugs again. Martin Kruze, public survivor of abuse and vocal advocate for children, was hurting and he was hiding his pain from virtually everyone. Kruze was going through his own private hell.

When Kruze started his crusade, he felt better than he had in years. It was more healing to him than anything else that had happened before. It wasn't enough for him to focus privately on his own recovery; he became the architect of a mission to end the abuse of children. That became his means to recovery. Every step he took and every word he spoke reached someone.

Survivors need to reach out, and they need to be reached. Sylvia Fraser did this every time she gave a reading from her book. There were people in the audience who wept in response. At first it felt good and it felt healing, but soon she stopped feeling anything herself. She saw that her public readings had become performances, which took away from "genuine healing on the inside." Sylvia Fraser stepped back into herself and into her writing world.

Martin Kruze had worked his plan almost to perfection. Stuckless and Roby had been arrested, and it was up to the criminal justice system to decide how great their punishment would be. By going to the police and media about his abuse, he had paved the way for a hundred men to come forward. He helped hundreds if not thousands more by putting his face and his words and his experiences into the public light as often as he could. In particular, he became a role model for male survivors. Apart from Sheldon Kennedy, they had no one else to compare themselves to. Now they could know that when they felt ugly and depressed and helpless, it was because of the abuse and not because they were sick or worthless.

But something wasn't quite right with Martin Kruze. His problems with depression and his addictions continued to plague him; even though he had taken every step he could to turn himself inside out—to purge himself of the shame and pain that he still carried. Maybe it was the uncertainty of leaving his abuser's fate in the hands of an impersonal "system." Or maybe it was, as some have suggested, that his story was starting to fade in the eyes of newspaper, TV, and radio reporters, who, after all, are paid to keep yesterday's news out of the spotlight.

Whatever the reason, Martin Kruze did not experience the cleansing he'd hoped for as he awaited Stuckless's outcome. He could only lie around on the couch and wait for the result as the demons he'd hoped to exorcise still churned away inside him.

I Would Draw a Picture of
a Shattered Mirror

MARQUE BRILL WAS SEXUALLY ABUSED when he was a child by a few men and an older youth who lived in his neighbourhood. He volunteered at CASAT and met Martin Kruze at the volunteer training. They were the only two men who attended, and both wanted to help in different ways. Kruze spoke publicly to raise awareness, promoted the handbook, and wrote letters for donations; Brill answered the phone, shipped the handbooks, and continues to wear a purple ribbon to raise awareness about child abuse.

I don't know that anyone would believe the weirdness that I go through when I'm by myself, because sometimes even I don't believe it. But sometimes that's part of the problem. It actually makes me quite dizzy when I know that my mind doesn't work as well as it should. I'm thinking that if I drew a picture of myself, I would draw a picture of a shattered mirror. Just out of the blue I start crying for no particular known reason when I'm by myself. One part of myself hardly believes that it's me that's crying; somebody else is crying. I don't actually feel myself crying. I'm looking at myself as if I was somebody else, and one part of me will be telling myself to stop pretending to cry.

*I can understand it in terms of self-programming
that happens after abuse, when it's no longer
something that you do willfully anymore. I mean,
it has its own program. You get used to hiding all
that stuff away, from, say, your family, so that
nobody knows what has happened to you. And,
thirty-odd years, or longer, down the road, it's
something that's actually rewired your neuro-
circuitry. But on the other hand, knowing that I
can know a lot of things about the whole process
intellectually doesn't really do a whole lot to
change the reality of what I have to put up with.
And what others have to put up with. And it takes
a lot of energy that I expend just going through
all this stuff, and I really do feel that it holds me
back from doing things that I feel that if I were
the person that I was meant to be, I'd be able
to do.*

*There's weird things, like sometimes I feel like I
have some horrible presence living inside me
that's totally separate from myself; I understand
that that's not necessarily an uncommon thing for
people in general, I guess, but it seems to be very
acute sometimes. There seems to be something
that really hates me . . . but it's not even a disgust
of myself that I could say that I actually even own,
it's something else that lives inside of me, who is*

really disgusted with me. Who finds me just totally disgusting, loathsome, and, I guess, really unbearable. And again, it's such a constant thing that always comes up and it gets worse as you get older, and it has its own life.

And it becomes necessary to shut yourself off from that because it's intolerable and the only way is to actually shut yourself down and that's what dissociation is, I suppose, in part. . . . It's quite excruciating. And it's not, as I say, a new thing for me either, perhaps not any big surprise, but it is, I mean a couple of years ago, when I did feel that, I felt that it was a revelation to think that I had a reason for feeling like this. And it was of some comfort to me at that point, and it has been of some comfort to me to think that I'm not just feeling like this because I'm an inherently weak and disgusting sort of person. But I've been having a lot more trouble retaining that belief of late. So, I do still continue to want to be able to do something in the area of prevention and I'm happy to be doing what I'm doing, because if this is what happens, if this is what someone has to live with, then I would like to do whatever I can, in whatever small way that I can to help to ensure that somebody else doesn't have to live with this, because it's not worth it.

CRIMINAL JUSTICE

No matter what happens, whatever the sentence is . . .
no one's ever going to give me back what I lost.
    —Gardens abuse survivor at Gordon
    Stuckless's sentencing hearing, 1997

ON SEPTEMBER 8, 1997, Gordon Stuckless appeared in court once more. This time he was there to plead guilty to twenty-four charges of sexual assault against twenty-four men. Because he had admitted to the offences, there would be no need for a trial to determine his innocence or guilt. Martin Kruze and the men who had come forward would no longer be "alleged victims." They would not have to get up on the stand and testify about the abuse that had been locked away in their minds and bodies for so long. They would not have to undergo cross-examination by Stuckless's defence lawyer, John Scarfe. Apart from Kruze, who had already been so open about his abuse, the men would now be released from any further public discussion or scrutiny—they could even try to put their abuse behind them if they wished. The burden of believing that they were responsible for causing and hiding the abuse was about to be lifted. By pleading guilty, Stuckless was taking responsibility for what he had done. Or at least what he was now on record for having done.

In the spring, Gordon Stuckless had been charged with fifty-seven charges against thirty-five men. Now, six months later, thirty-three charges had been withdrawn. According to Detective Tredrea, a deal was struck "in the interest of saving thirty-five guys from going through the torment of testifying."

The "deal" was this: Ten of the original thirty-five men had told the police that in addition to the acts of abuse that had been widely reported in the press—assaults that involved touching, masturbation, and oral sex—Stuckless had also penetrated them. From a legal standpoint, penetration is considered a more serious offence, so it involves more serious charges. "Unfortunately, in the eyes of the law, when the penetration type of offences occur, the [penalty] goes way up," said Tredrea, who characterized this stage of the prosecution as a "balancing act." In a move typical of the plea-bargaining process, Stuckless agreed to admit to the lesser offences, but he wouldn't admit to the "more serious" ones. Had they proceeded to trial, the latter charges would have been included.

Many men and women who have been sexually assaulted recoil at the thought that charges of abuse could ever be considered "more" or "less" serious. They are adamant that nobody can measure the gravity of an offence based on the specific act.

How, they wonder, can the criminal justice system presume that an assault involving sexual intercourse is necessarily worse than a child's being forced to perform oral sex on someone or having his or her penis, buttocks, or vulva stroked when the child is trying to sleep in his or her bed?

In Stuckless's case, according to Detective Tredrea, the police and the Crown attorneys believed, based on the sheer number of victims alone, that justice would be served even with the plea bargain. The *Globe and Mail* succinctly summed up this stage of the process: "the Crown simply brought to court the [charges] that were readily provable." If the victims could be spared the ordeal of testifying and being cross-examined by Stuckless's lawyer, it would be in the men's best interests to have Stuckless plead guilty to the lesser charges.

Unlike the actions of John Paul Roby, who entered a plea of not guilty and later went to trial, Stuckless's specific acts of abuse against the now twenty-four men received limited scrutiny. According to Tredrea, police went through the Roby investigation with a "fine-toothed comb"; Stuckless wasn't put under the same "magnifying glass" because he pleaded guilty. Instead, the Crown and Gordon Stuckless's lawyer prepared a "statement of fact" agreed to by both the Crown and the defence. The statement described what methods Stuckless had used to befriend or entice the boys, what he had done to the boys, and what the effects of the abuse had been on the boys. Gordon Stuckless's twenty-year career of selecting, befriending, manipulating, tricking, betraying, sexually abusing, and silencing boys—six hundred acts of crime that were now on public record—was summarized in a four-paragraph statement:

> He [Stuckless] would begin by befriending them. In some cases he would also befriend the parents of the victims, thus gaining their [the parents'] trust. The parents would allow the victims to go to hockey games and movies with the accused. In other cases, he would befriend the victims and gain their trust by allowing them into Maple Leaf Gardens for Toronto Maple Leaf practices, and for Toronto Toros and Toronto Marlies hockey games. He would take the victims to movies, buy them meals or give them hockey sticks or other memorabilia. Many of the children whom Stuckless abused came from low-income families in Regent Park.
>
> The sexual conduct with the boys included fondling them; performing oral sex on them; having them perform oral sex on him; masturbating them; having them masturbate him; masturbating in front of them; mutual masturbation; rubbing against them until he ejaculated; having the boys perform sexual acts with each other in front of him and his Maple Leaf Gardens supervisor, George Hannah, while he and Hannah masturbated; having the boys perform oral sex on George Hannah; and participating with Hannah in group sex with the boys.

*The relationships with the boys lasted anywhere
from several days to several months or several years.
They took place in a variety of locations, including
Maple Leaf Gardens, the boys' homes, movie theatres,
classrooms, showers, cars, Cherry Beach [in Toronto's
east end] and Stuckless's home.*

*The various impacts of the abuse on the victims
included depression, loneliness, trauma, shame, pain,
guilt, nightmares, helplessness, fear, loss of confidence,
rage and self-hatred. Some quit school, developed a
dependency on drugs and alcohol, had difficulties in
developing and maintaining personal relationships,
or required extensive counselling, all of which impaired
their ability to get or keep a job. Many felt their lives
had been ruined. There were several suicide attempts.*

The "statement of fact" did describe what many of the men
had experienced. Gordon Stuckless had done everything it said
and the effects were as stated—and yet none of it seemed to adequately capture the intensity of the relationships he created, the
depths of the betrayal, the life-altering consequences, and the
shock and horror the boys experienced when Stuckless took
their friendship and trust, their whole beings, and skewered
them. The absolute power that he held over the boys, the threats
he used, and his particular way of comforting the boys by telling
them that "everything was going to be all right," as well as his
acts of anal rape—these and more no longer existed.

After Stuckless had pleaded guilty and the agreement about what had happened was struck, the only step remaining was for Justice David Watt to determine Gordon Stuckless's sentence. The sentencing hearing was scheduled for October 10.

The courts consider many variables in sentencing for sexual assault: Was the offender in a position of authority or trust? Were threats used? Were weapons used? Were there physical injuries? Although sexual assault carries a maximum penitentiary sentence of ten years, sentence length is more often less than two years. When there is more than one victim, the sentence is expected to be longer.

The sentencing hearing for Gordon Stuckless was described in the press as "dramatic and often emotional"—but these terms do not convey the bald anger and calm despair that alternately punctuated the hearing. All of the men had been asked to write victim impact statements, using their own words to describe how the abuse had affected their lives. They were also given the option of reading their statements aloud in court. Because Stuckless entered a guilty plea, none of them had to testify against him, and only a few, along with Martin Kruze, had spoken on record with the media. Thus, this would be the only time that they would be able to speak in an official setting about their abuse—if they wanted to. Many did complete statements; some threw them away because they didn't think what they had to say would make a difference.

Eight men chose to read them aloud. To everyone's surprise, Martin Kruze did not. He and his father met with the Crown attorneys ahead of time and decided that because he had not been feeling well and because he had spoken so much already, he shouldn't feel any further obligation to speak at the hearing. For once, Martin Kruze didn't want to speak. Instead, he sat quietly while the others spoke of how profoundly the abuse had affected their lives. Their experiences were eerily similar to those that Kruze had voiced in the months before—shame, depression, feelings of worthlessness, drug and alcohol abuse, problems with relationships, poverty and unemployment, and so on.

They also spoke of the effect that their abuse had on their children's lives. One after another they despaired about how the abuse infected their relationships with their children and how their own children were now being damaged: the men couldn't touch or hug them for fear that such gestures would somehow lead to abuse or that others would suspect them of abuse. Unable to protect themselves when they were children, they believed they wouldn't be able to protect their children, so they restricted their lives: no sports, no hockey, no after school activities, no overnights at friends. One man was so paralyzed by the thought of what could happen to his own child that on the day his son was born he couldn't even hold him.

Much of the anger was aimed directly at Gordon Stuckless. Reports from the *Globe and Mail* recount how an "athletic-looking man stared angrily at Stuckless, slumped in his chair as he listened to the testimony. 'No matter what happens, whatever the sentence is . . . no one's ever going to give me back what I lost,'" said the man. Another could only express his regret: 'I forgive Mr. Stuckless, but I can't forget. And I wish with all my heart it didn't happen.'"

The court also heard the testimony of Dr. Peter Collins, a psychiatrist from the Clarke Institute of Psychiatry in Toronto who had evaluated Gordon Stuckless. Collins had previously assessed and treated Stuckless, the first time in 1995, when he had pleaded guilty to another set of charges involving the sexual abuse of children. Collins was also aware that Stuckless had been involved in group treatment at the Clarke Institute as a result of an even earlier conviction for similar offences in 1988 and that Stuckless had participated in treatment at the Ontario Correctional Institute in 1996. Stuckless had agreed to go on sex-drive-reduction medication and, ironically, was slated to see Dr. Collins to begin taking the drugs just a few days after he was arrested in February.

After extensive testing, Collins determined that in clinical terms Gordon Stuckless was a pedophile and a hebephile. The first is defined as having an erotic preference for children and the second as having an erotic preference for children who have reached puberty. Both are considered life-long conditions with no known cures. Managing and treating pedophiles and hebephiles therefore involves assessing and weighing factors that increase the individual's chances of re-offending against factors that decrease that likelihood. Admitting that one is a pedophile and being willing to engage in treatment decrease the likelihood of re-offending. According to Dr. Collins's testimony, individual counselling, medication that reduces sex drive, and participation in relapse-prevention groups are the mainstay of treatment. Indeed, Stuckless had already begun this treatment, on the advice of Collins, when Kruze blew the whistle on him.

The question of what to do with pedophiles elicits strong and contradictory responses. Some of Stuckless's victims were adamant: he should be drawn, quartered, and hung. Some thought that even hanging him would be too kind—they wanted him to experience every bit of pain that they'd endured, and they wanted him to live the rest of his life in prison, surrounded by men who would hate, threaten, and sexually assault him. Others saw killing or inflicting pain on him as replicating what he did to them—and that just means more abuse. But many were skeptical of the idea that pedophiles can be "treated." As living proof of how easily and completely a pedophile can infiltrate, manipulate, and destroy people's lives by the score, these victims wondered: If Gordon Stuckless and George Hannah could manipulate Maple Leaf Gardens for their own purposes, why couldn't they use the same tricks to outfox any system set up to "help" them?

William Marshall, a forensic psychologist and professor at Queen's University in Kingston, Ontario, works with sex offenders at the Bath Institution, a medium-security prison near Kingston. Marshall doesn't even like the word "pedophile." "It's an objectionable word," says Marshall, "because it literally means 'child-lover.' And these guys don't love children—at least what they do does not reflect a love of children.

Some claim to love the child but you hardly do this sort of thing if you genuinely do love them. It's done out of self-interest."

Marshall says that the term shouldn't be used to describe men who use coercion, trickery, and manipulation to achieve sexual relations with a youngster. Instead, he prefers the term "child molester." Some people feel that even the term "child molester" is not strong enough. One man who was assaulted by George Hannah in the Leafs dressing room laughs derisively when he hears the term "child molester." "That's a nice, sugar-coated way of saying it—doesn't that sound nice," he says. "Rapists—that's what they are. That's what Hannah did to me. He raped me."

Marshall, who works in conjunction with the Correctional Service of Canada, notes that over the past decade there has been a shift in the way the federal penitentiary system deals with sex offenders. Whereas therapy was previously provided for only the most psychotic and disturbed of offenders, there are now some services available for most offenders. He says that the overall goal is "not only to lock them up in jail for a long time but to rehabilitate them somehow." Such rehabilitation has the overall goal of limiting, as much as possible, the risk that child molesters will re-offend. According to Marshall, the prevailing view among psychiatrists—and the general public for that matter—is that pedophiles, or what he calls child molesters, cannot be treated. "That's just flat-out not true," he says. "The evidence is as clear as can be that they are amenable to treatment. They might be a little more difficult to treat, but they do respond to it. People want to monsterize them, so that they feel a sense of relief and can say they don't belong to our species. But we'd never be able to treat them if they were truly freaks."

To measure the success of rehabilitation, statistics are kept on repeat offences after the men are released from prison. Marshall says that the recidivism rate among the men he works with at the Bath prison is about 3 per cent when they follow up with men who have been released into society for more than four years. "The fact is, we have these guys sitting in the prison system," he says, "and they are going to be released some day. If we don't at least try to do something with them, they are going to get out and do the same damn thing."

Martin Kruze's friend Art Lockhart also has ideas about what to do with sex offenders. Lockhart teaches criminal justice studies at Humber College in Toronto and agrees that the overriding question is, "How do you stop the behaviour?" It's also important to ask what the offender "is capable of doing as opposed to looking at them and saying 'You're an evil monster. We're going to put you away forever.' Because the fact of the matter is everybody gets out. The percentage of people who stay in custody for their entire lives is less than half a per cent." As long as we demonize men who molest children, we're contributing to the conditions that supported their offending behaviour in the first place. Lockhart is interested in models of justice that restore dignity and self-worth to everyone involved, in which the process revolves around creating conditions for the people who have been victimized to confront their abusers if they want to and to feel heard and to have their strength and power validated. "They will express that some very powerful things happen," says Lockhart. "People say that for the first time 'I have been heard.' For the first time, 'I'm not looked upon as somebody who brought this on myself. I'm a powerful person.' "

Lockhart is also interested in processes that build on each offender's strengths and work from the question "What do we need to do to help this person stop offending?" as opposed to "How long can we put him away for?" Lockhart is convinced that as long as we focus on arresting, convicting, and incarcerating, we will not meet the needs of victims and we will not truly stop the behaviour of child molesters.

During Gordon Stuckless's one-day hearing, the Crown and the defence made their sentencing recommendations. Crown prosecutor Jim Hughes recommended the maximum, a sentence of ten years in prison, characterizing Stuckless's actions as "a massive crime, involving many acts with many individuals over many years." Hughes said Stuckless had used his position as a minor hockey coach and his job at the Gardens to gain the trust of his victims and their parents and then to lure the boys into being sexually assaulted. "It [that trust] enabled him to assault them without using an iron fist," Hughes said. Further, he stated, this particular form of coercion was one of the very strategies that Stuckless used to secure his victims' silence: "It also makes them complicit . . . it makes them unable to tell." How does anyone tell about something that on the face of things doesn't seem to hurt and is being done by someone who is liked and respected by the child and his family? Gordon Stuckless's iron fist was well hidden from everyone.

Gordon Stuckless's lawyer, John Scarfe, recommended a sentence of four to five years, arguing that Stuckless had taken responsibility for his actions, had already made progress in a treatment program for sex offenders, and was willing to be "chemically castrated" by taking drugs to reduce his sex drive. The *Toronto Star* reported that Scarfe said, "The accused has demonstrated unusual remorse for his actions." Scarfe then read from a letter of apology that Stuckless had written to all of his victims: "How do I say I'm sorry for all the shame and humiliation I have caused? The word sorry is not enough."

With all of the evidence at his disposal from the sentencing hearing, it was now up to Justice David Watt to determine how long Gordon Stuckless would be sentenced for the crimes he committed against twenty-four men.

On October 27, Gordon Stuckless appeared in court to receive his sentence. Many of the victims were present. Once again Martin Kruze surprised everyone—he did not even attend the final session of the process that he had ignited eight months before. His physical and mental condition would not allow him to be there. The men who did attend hung on every word as Justice Watt gave a long, explicit, and articulate rationale for his determination.

According to the records, Watt was convinced that Stuckless "consistently and without apparent hesitation, violated the trust reposed in him...his conduct was purposeful, his approach predatory. He had but one goal in mind. The boys were merely means to an end, the sexual gratification of Gordon Stuckless."

Justice Watt also commented on the systematic nature of Stuckless's abuse. "[T]he crimes of Gordon Stuckless were an integral part of an overall scheme of defilement. They were not situational, momentary lapses of judgement, when reason was temporarily dethroned. They were, rather, carefully orchestrated, deliberate and predatory," Watt stated. "For nearly two decades, Gordon Stuckless routinely targeted and cultivated more than two dozen naive, often disadvantaged boys to satisfy his own sexual fantasies and desires. Equally routinely, he violated a position of authority and a trust he had so assiduously created and sedulously fostered. He was indifferent to his victims, unaware and uncaring of the effects, immediate and long term, on those whom he had victimized."

Watt's assessment of Gordon Stuckless's behaviour was dead on: he regarded it as predatory—designed to procure boys for his own consumption. But Watt emphasized that Stuckless "neither caused nor threatened actual bodily harm...apart from the coercion which is implicit in conduct which takes place in the context of any relationship where there is a power imbalance." Consequently, Watt said, the maximum punishment of ten years that the Crown prosecutors were seeking was not realistic, because "the crimes of Gordon Stuckless are nearer to the lower end of the spectrum."

Justice Watt also noted that Stuckless had not been charged with having anal intercourse with any of the men who had reported being abused by him, and he had not used weapons to exert (or threaten to exert) force on the abused. "It should also be made clear that Gordon Stuckless is being sentenced for what he did, not where he did it," Watt stated. "He doesn't get more [jail time] because he worked at Maple Leaf Gardens or committed some of his offences there. Neither does he get less. The publicity accorded this offender and his offences does not change the nature of the offence, or the circumstances of the offender. It does not make the crime more serious nor the offender more dangerous."

Watt took into account several other factors as well: Stuckless had pleaded guilty to twenty-four charges against him, had acknowledged the harm he'd done to his victims and shown remorse, had agreed to take medication to manage his condition, and, perhaps most important, was, for all legal intents and purposes, being tried as a first-time offender for his crimes—these crimes pre-dated the ones he had already been convicted of and therefore had to be viewed as his first. He had also been incarcerated for eight months while awaiting prosecution.

Watt concluded that in a case like Stuckless's, greater societal good would be accomplished not by having him serve a lengthy jail term—such as three or four years—but rather by a shorter incarceration followed by a "post-release scheme that ensures supervision, punishes failure to comply, assists in rehabilitation and provides a longer period of control albeit not within prison venues." In recommending this "blended sentence" Watt added that he was concerned about the "unthinking, retributive imposition of inflated terms of imprisonment [which] has an immediate and visible effect, yet when it is done, it offers little or no protection for society. The goal of sentencing is not achieved when the offender walks out of jail at the end of the term, untreated."

With all of this in mind, Justice Watt handed down the sentence: two years less a day in an Ontario reformatory, followed by three years' probation with regular reports to a probation officer. The sentence was actually shorter than the one recommended by Stuckless's own defence lawyer. The decision was based on the aforementioned three- to four-year jail term that Watt believed was best blended with out-of-incarceration supervision, minus the eight months Stuckless had already spent in jail. Further conditions held that Stuckless had to remain in Ontario unless he received written permission from the court or his probation officer to venture outside the province and that he continue to be treated by Dr. Collins or his designate and submit to the sex-drive-reduction medication. Stuckless's sentence also prevented him from ever being on or near any "public park, recreational facility, day care centre, schoolyard, playground or community centre where persons under the age of 14 are, or may reasonably be expected to be present." Finally, Stuckless was prevented from seeking any kind of paid or volunteer position "in a capacity that involves being in a position of trust or authority towards persons under 14 years of age."

Regardless of how well Justice Watt had understood the predatory intent and actions of Gordon Stuckless and no matter how thoughtfully he had constructed the corresponding sentence, the men sitting in the court, listening to his carefully recited reasons, heard only two things: Gordon Stuckless's crimes were on the "lesser end" of the spectrum, and he was being sentenced to two years less a day. The verdict was shocking to virtually everyone in the courtroom. Men who had shaken every time they had come to court and men who had wept quietly were now devastated and enraged. Justice Watt had done to them what Stuckless had done twenty years earlier: he had betrayed them. The men shouted and wept as they rose to their feet, and many stormed out of the courtroom. It was especially galling for them to hear Justice Watt state that because there had been no anal penetration, physical violence, or threat of violence, Stuckless's crime wasn't violent. As survivor Derek Goodyear says, "Well, unless Judge Watt is in our boots, or walked a mile in our shoes, he doesn't know if it's violent or not. Gordon Stuckless took away our trust, and that was a key thing, our trust. . . . Once an adult breaks that trust, takes away our ability to trust anymore, how are we supposed to trust anyone again? And then Justice Watt just slapped us in the face again. [He said,] 'Well, I'm a judge, don't trust me.'"

Goodyear and the other men realized that if it was hurting them this much, it would be an even more terrible blow for Martin Kruze, because he had stuck his neck out so far.

Stuckless had abused every one of them, but it was Kruze they believed would be most humiliated by a sentence that, to them, amounted to a slap on the wrist for Gordon Stuckless.

THE SENTENCE WAS A SLAP IN THE FACE

FOR MANY OF THE SURVIVORS of sexual abuse and their families, hearing the sentence given to Gordon Stuckless was like being abused all over again.

> I look at our system and all these lawyers and people as shit, 'cause they make me a victim of stolen life here on earth. —Brian Silber

> How many people, like in the courtroom that day, how many people looked at those guys as twelve- and thirteen-year-olds? I bet most of them looked at them as thirty-year-old guys, or whatever age they were. —Barry Bingham

> Change the system. If you abuse a child, it's the same as if you actually assaulted a child with a closed fist and you gave him a punch in the mouth. You murdered her soul and that's what it is. That's what happened to me, that's the way I felt. I felt as though he had murdered my soul. So when they first passed sentence on him, and they gave him two years less a day, with a year time served, I thought, "What in the fuck is the matter with them?" ... I lived through twenty-three years of hell. What, for him to do it to another kid? —Ken Comeau

The sentence that came down was a slap in the face to us all, especially, I believe, to Martin because Martin was the one; he stuck his neck out by going in front of all the media. Taking that first huge, huge step in opening the door for the rest of us to be able to come forward. —Derek Goodyear

Degrading. It was degrading to me. Why did I come out in the open to find out that he was only going to get two years and a promise to take a pill? —Steve Sutton

Well, there was no violence! What do you mean, violence? I thought violence against children by any means was violence. Whether you abuse them, whether you slap them, whether you yell at them. . . . But no, our society doesn't look at it like that, our criminal system doesn't look at child abuse as all that bad. Oh, they're kids, they'll get over it, they probably think. Yeah, we'll get over it, yeah. You know when I'll get over it? When I'm dead and gone. That's when I'll get over it. —Ken Comeau

9

ENDING IT ALL

I want to die and I am going to jump. I've just had
enough. I've had enough of everything.
    —Martin Kruze, October 1997

MARTIN KRUZE HEARD ABOUT the Stuckless sentence the same
way that the public did: on the news. Lying on the couch at
home, he heard and saw on the radio and television news
reports later that day that because Gordon Stuckless's crimes
did not include acts of anal penetration, violence, or threats of
violence, Justice Watt had deemed them to be of a less serious
nature than those deserving the maximum sentence for sexual
abuse. Kruze heard that many of his fellow survivors reacted in
anger and stormed out of the courthouse accusing Justice Watt
of betraying them all over again. He also heard that many of the
men cried and comforted one another outside the courthouse.

    Even if he had wanted to attend what should have been
the final chapter in the case against Gordon Stuckless—the final

chapter of the story that Kruze so dramatically brought to public life—he wasn't able to. For weeks now, he had been feeling more and more depressed. He didn't seem to have any strength or energy—he was losing himself and he was losing his will to live.

Kruze almost did not live to find out the results of the Stuckless sentencing. On Friday, October 24, he had perched on the railing of the Leaside Bridge, one of a series of bridges that cross over the Don Valley Parkway and the Don River. Every day these bridges take commuters east and west, back and forth across the city. While many people drive, others cycle and walk the long stretches of these bridges as well. According to a report in the *Toronto Sun,* that day, a passerby on the Leaside Bridge saw Kruze up on the railing and, terrified that he was going to jump, called the police. Minutes later Police Constable Mike Jenkins arrived.

Kruze had moved farther down the bridge and beckoned to him. As Jenkins approached, Martin said, "I want to die and I am going to jump. I've just had enough. I've had enough of everything."

When Jenkins tackled him to stop him from going over the railing, Kruze didn't put up a fight. "I don't want to hurt you," he said. "I just want to die." Jenkins helped him off the bridge and took him to Toronto East General Hospital. The hospital staff tried to get Kruze to admit himself voluntarily, but he wouldn't. Jenkins stressed that he had just pulled him off the ledge of a bridge, so the hospital decided to admit him as an "involuntary admission," because he was deemed to be a threat to himself.

Kruze was now exactly where he had been so many times before—sitting in a hospital. All the "therapy" that his speaking out had done for him, all the satisfaction that he felt when the other survivors came forward and Gordon Stuckless was arrested and charged—all that had happened between February 18 and now—was gone. Any empowerment that he had felt during that time, any control that he felt that he had taken to help himself, now ceased to exist. He was sitting in a hospital where he was saying he didn't want to be, and yet the hospital seemed to offer him the only protection he had from himself. Martin Kruze had spent much of his life feeling the harm that others had done to him, but he had also spent some of that time intent on harming himself. This was another one of those times.

Kruze was scheduled to be discharged three days later—the same day that Gordon Stuckless was to receive his sentence: Monday, October 27. Astrida and Gary visited Martin in hospital that weekend. They had never seen him in such a state before—he was nervous and shaking. All they could do was sit with him and listen to him. For the first time, they heard Martin say, "This is the end of me." When they asked him what he meant, he was overcome by tears and couldn't talk.

Gary was even more worried about Martin and the timing of his release from hospital. He telephoned and pleaded with the psychiatrist to keep him in longer. The psychiatrist told him that Martin would not "act it out" and that considering his numerous and mostly unsuccessful stints in hospitals, Martin was "abusing the system as always."

Martin Kruze was discharged as planned from Toronto East General Hospital on October 27. When Jayne arrived to pick him up, she was heartened at first. He seemed to be his old, calm self, "back to being my Martin," she says. After getting him settled in their apartment, and after repeated assurances from Martin that he was feeling fine, Jayne went off to work, as she always did. Her catering schedule kept her working all the time, no matter what shape Martin—or she, for that matter—was in.

Jayne remembers the day clearly: "At that point I was extremely stressed out. But when he came home from hospital, I was very relieved. I thought he was feeling better and not so depressed." Even though she had been through this cycle with him many times before, seeing Martin feeling better became all that Jayne needed to believe that he would be all right.

But when she returned from work in the early afternoon, Jayne soon learned that everything was not all right. Martin looked as though he had a rash on his neck, and he was red in the face. Jayne figured that he was having some kind of reaction to the Prozac he'd received the past weekend at the hospital.

When Jayne tried to reach the physician who had treated Martin at the East General, to ask about what seemed to be a reaction to the medication, the doctor refused to speak to her, having only dealt "officially" with Martin's brother Gary. Jayne could hear the doctor instructing the person she was speaking to, to "tell her to go to a pharmacy" if she thought Martin was having problems with the medication.

Jayne was scared and didn't know what to do. She didn't call

Gary or anyone else, and she had to get back to work. She told Martin that she had to go back out again and asked him if he would be okay if she left him for a couple of hours. He said yes, but when she came back, his face was still red and she was sure that the reaction to the medication was getting worse.

The problem wasn't the medication, Martin told her. The truth of the matter—and the explanation for the red face and neck rash—was that he had tried to kill himself again. This time he had tried to choke himself to death with one of Jayne's scarves.

It's hard for Jayne to recall these last days with Martin without breaking down. When she relates what was happening to him and how she was trying to help, you can't help but feel that she was doing the best she could. So overwhelmed was she by Martin's state that Jayne herself was at her wits' end. What do you do when the person you love seems to want only to die? What do you do when the "help" doesn't seem to make any difference or really doesn't even seem to be there at all? Jayne's own isolation and desperation was so complete that she no longer knew how to get help for Martin. Although many people would later say they would have done anything and everything to help Martin Kruze, Jayne could think of no one who could help.

Finally Jayne contacted her own doctor and pleaded for help. Since Martin had been released from Toronto East General just a short time before—and seemed to have been in the care of a physician there who wasn't going to help anyway—she begged to have him admitted to Toronto Western, a request to which her doctor agreed.

Soon Jayne was driving Martin to Toronto Western. "It's funny," Jayne recalls, "but walking down the street to the hospital, Martin wanted to tell me something, and I asked him if he wanted to go into the hospital cafeteria and talk about it—but he didn't. And he never did tell me what he wanted, but I think it was that he did not want to live."

Martin—who was back to feeling severely depressed—sat with Jayne in the hospital until two o'clock in the morning, "waiting for some psychiatrist to tell us the same old garbage that they told us every time," Jayne says. Having been working long hours, not eating properly, and in general feeling that she could not cope anymore, Jayne felt as though she had nothing more to give.

"I remember looking at him, with his little boy face; he was in such pain—I will never forget it," she recalls, in tears. "I pleaded with the doctor to keep him in the hospital, but they did not want to. I just pleaded and pleaded, and Martin was just sitting there. He was in such bad shape. He was just so scared."

The psychiatric staff at last agreed to keep Martin in hospital overnight for observation. When Jayne called from work early the next day, the attending psychiatrist told her that a new team of doctors would be coming on duty that morning and they would decide if he should remain in hospital. Around ten o'clock that morning, Martin himself called and told her, "They're kicking me out."

Once again, though, when Jayne came to pick him up, Martin seemed to be in his old, cheerful state, acting much more calmly than the night before. Again, Jayne brought him home, and after receiving assurances that he was feeling fine, she went back to work. Later, when she spoke to him on the phone, Martin said that he had been chatting with his brothers and everything was fine. Martin said he wasn't having suicidal thoughts; that phase, he told Jayne, had passed. Jayne was relieved.

That same evening Martin's father and his wife, Mara, stopped in at Martin and Jayne's apartment. Imants had been worried about his son and had been calling all over the city looking for him. He didn't expect to find him at home, but there he was, sitting calmly in his apartment. They headed out to the local Second Cup coffee shop for a coffee, and Martin tapped his fingers on the table to the rhythm of the South American music. Always the drummer, his father thought. Later he hugged his son good night and handed over $100—something Kruze regularly asked for and got from his father and every other family member. Imants remembers that Martin's hug felt weak, as if he weren't there. Imants nudged him to try harder to hug him, and Martin did. Much later that night Jayne arrived home. Martin was already in bed reading from the Bible that he kept near the bed.

The next morning, Martin and Jayne woke early. Jayne was in the habit of rising at five o'clock to prepare for work, and Martin got up with her and smoked a cigarette while the two talked. Jayne left their apartment around seven o'clock, promising to call him from work. Martin called her first, around ten o'clock. "He sounded fine," says Jayne. "I remember him saying, 'I just wanted to hear your voice.'" Jayne suggested he go for a nice long walk in the park not far from their home near Casa Loma, and he said that that sounded good. At the end of the conversation Martin said, "I love you and I'll see you later."

It was the last time anybody would ever talk to Martin Kruze.

He did go for his walk, but he pointed himself in the direction of the Bloor Street Viaduct—the one that writer Michael Ondaatje says "lounges" south of the Leaside Bridge and that carries not only cars, cyclists, and pedestrians but also one of Toronto's subway lines. The Bloor Street Viaduct, graceful and majestic, was christened the Prince Edward when it was built in 1918. It is one of several bridges around the world considered to be a "magnet" for suicidal people. People who live in the Riverdale area to the east of the bridge almost can't go anywhere without crossing it. Astrida was near it that day when she went to get her groceries, and Gary and Teresa each made separate trips across it on their way to work.

On this bright sunny Thursday morning, as cars sped past and pedestrians made the long trek across the bridge, Martin Kruze climbed up onto the railing. In contrast to every other time, when he waited or called out for help, this time he yelled to two people passing by. "Watch me!" he shouted. And then he stepped off the railing.

You Have This Intense Feeling of Abandonment

KRUZE'S SUICIDE WAS devastating for many survivors of sexual abuse.

> *I can understand, because I've tried to kill myself*
> *three times. I did the drug scene, I did the alcohol*
> *scene. And the biggest fear for me, if I did end up*
> *killing myself, is my family that's gotta go through*
> *it, not me, 'cause it's ended for me. It's my family*
> *that has to live the rest of their lives with it. You*
> *know it's almost like [Gordon Stuckless] had actu-*
> *ally murdered us, because he murdered my soul. I*
> *had no childhood, none that I could actually say*
> *that I enjoyed, because there's no part of my child-*
> *hood that I actually enjoyed. And that's something*
> *I'll never get back.* —Ken Comeau

> *You have this intense feeling of abandonment.*
> *Abandonment is really not the right word. It's used*
> *a lot, and I've used it a lot, but even as I say it*
> *right now, I realize that it's not enough. You have*
> *this feeling of aloneness, you know, like of intense*
> *separateness from every other person and it's*
> *almost like being covered in cellophane, where*
> *you can't really feel anybody. And nobody can*

really quite hear you. You know, it's over. It's done with, the damage has been done. So what can you do? So what do you do? You've got to stand up on a bridge, jump off, and let everybody know. "Please watch me. See, this is me. This is my life. This is all I'm worth. That's it." So that's what he does. I mean, I imagine that, that's just almost predictable. —Steven Haylestrom

And the fact that because Martin did stick his neck out on the line, that he couldn't handle it anymore and that he figured, "Well, I just got assaulted again, but this time by a judge." But again, I don't know exactly what was going through Martin's mind, I can only presume because of knowing what has gone through my mind when I've attempted in the past. The fact of "There's no sense in me being here. Let's just end it all right now." —Derek Goodyear

10

DEATH'S AFTERMATH

I wanted somebody to deny that this had happened.
—Gordon Kirke, 1997

ALL AFTERNOON JAYNE HAD had a nagging feeling she couldn't quite figure out. Hours later, after she finished cleaning up from her catering job, she climbed into her van to head home. For some reason she decided to call Martin's oldest brother, Ron, who was now living in North Carolina. She had never met him, yet she pulled her van over to the side of the road and decided to call him right then and there. And that was how Jayne heard the terrible news. It turned out that by this time the police had contacted Imants, and he called Astrida to break the news to her.

Devastated, she called Ron and left frantic messages on Gary and Teresa's voicemail. They were both at work and no one could reach them directly. As soon as Teresa arrived home and heard the sound of Astrida's voice, she knew that something awful had happened and rushed over to Astrida's.

In the meantime, Gary was listening to the radio in his car as he drove to a business appointment and heard the news headline that the man at the centre of the Gardens sex scandal was dead. "Please, God, no!" Gary said and for the next ten minutes hung onto every commercial and news headline until the station followed up on the story. Because media interest was so intense, the network violated the police request not to release Kruze's identity until all the family members had been notified, and so Gary heard the news on the radio that his brother had killed himself.

Everyone was trying to reach Jayne—the police, Jane Hawtin—and with nerves frayed from weeks and months of worry about Martin, Jayne says that the only word to describe her state upon hearing the news from Ron was "devastated, just devastated." Even so, Jayne didn't call anyone to come and help her deal with her shock and grief; she pulled herself together and drove home alone to the apartment she had shared with Martin. Later that night she drove—alone again—up to stay with her mother.

Meanwhile, Detective Tredrea took Imants to identify his son's body at the morgue, and by that night, the Kruzes were assembling at the home of Martin's mother, Astrida.

On the very day that Kruze committed suicide, fellow survivor Derek Goodyear also came close to killing himself. He was due to start his shift at two o'clock in the afternoon at the warehouse where he was employed as a forklift operator and was making his daily drive west along Derry Road in Brampton, Ontario, just west of Toronto. There was an ache in the pit of his stomach.

Abruptly, he pulled his van over to the side of the road where Derry crosses over Highway 410. Before he knew it, he was out of his van, standing on the edge of the bridge, ready to jump.

To this day, he's not entirely sure what happened next. "It was like something pushed me in the chest, pushed me back," he remembers. "I literally fell back off the railing, onto the bridge. Then all of a sudden, I just shook my head, got in my van, and drove to work."

When he arrived at his job, Goodyear broke down. Although he was able to pull himself together and wipe away his tears, he couldn't concentrate. He just wasn't able to get the forklift to move crates the way he had done a hundred times before.

Goodyear's boss could see that he was having trouble at work. He suggested that Derek leave early and take the next couple of days off. Derek headed home: he wanted to see his kids. Even though they were already asleep, he needed to kiss them and tell them that he loved them. When he came back down the stairs, his wife (at the time) asked him to sit down because she had some bad news for him. "All the emotions just started going right through me," he said after he heard. "My wife could see how hurt and bent out of shape I was so I didn't dare tell her that I had tried to take my life that day too. I find it very scary and in some ways ironic that the day I'm ready to take the jump, Martin did."

The staff of the *Jane Hawtin Live* show had been trying to find Martin Kruze that day and for several days before. They had his home phone number, his pager number, the catering

business number, but they couldn't reach him or Jayne anywhere. Knowing him to be an enthusiastic guest, they were
puzzled that he had not answered their voice messages trying to
book him for that day's show for a panel discussion on sex
offenders and the Stuckless sentence. Barry Bingham was on his
way down to be a guest on the show. When a tip came in that
afternoon that someone had died after jumping from the Bloor
Street Viaduct, they immediately feared the worst. When it was
confirmed, Jane Hawtin—upset herself—had to break the news
to Bingham, who was now waiting in the Green Room for the
show to start. Barry's own son Darryl had been abused by
Gordon Stuckless almost ten years earlier, and now Martin
Kruze had killed himself. Barry felt sick about Martin and now
he was worried about his son.

Maple Leaf Gardens was also reacting to the news of Martin
Kruze's death. When Ken Dryden, president and general manager of the Toronto Maple Leafs, got a call telling him that
Kruze had killed himself, he first thought, "Why did it happen?
What must it have been like? Why now?" But his initial shock
was followed by a series of more practical concerns—the press
would soon be calling. "What does one say?" he recalls asking
himself. "Do you issue a press release? All you know is that the
person at the other end of the line is probably not going to
believe you, is going to be very aggressive, and you're going to
get questions like, 'Do you feel responsible?' What do you say?
And what do you say when it's all of a sudden, and you've never
thought about these things before, and you know that a few

hundred thousand people are either going to read it, or hear it
or watch it on television. No matter what's going to happen,
you're going to look like an idiot. And that's the base line of the
whole thing: you're an idiot. Now the question is, how much of
an idiot are you going to be?" For the man famed for anticipat-
ing shots with a steady and collected calm, there had been no
practice for this one.

With the responsibilities of moving into his new job as head
of the Leafs organization, Dryden had also never gotten around
to answering the letter that sat somewhere in a pile on his desk.
Addressed to team owner Steve Stavro, it had been passed on to
Dryden in late August. It was Martin Kruze's letter asking Maple
Leaf Gardens to donate money to produce additional copies of
the handbook that he had been championing in his volunteer
work for CASAT. Dryden had never figured out how to respond
to Kruze's request, and now time had run out. Dryden knew
that he had to do something, but he wasn't quite sure what.

On the one hand, it was obvious that there needed to be
some kind of official reaction to the suicide and some sort of
follow-up to assure the public that steps were being taken so
that the abuse that Kruze and many other men had suffered
would never happen again. On the other hand, the organization had never publicly admitted that the abuse had taken place
on its premises and no one knew what steps, if any, had been
taken to address Kruze's original concerns that sexual abuse was
still taking place at Maple Leaf Gardens.

At the urging of Ken and Lynda Dryden, the organization

has since put on a series of forums on child sexual abuse, orig-
inally holding them at the Gardens and then at the Delta
Chelsea hotel downtown. But the ones organized for adults,
no matter how inspiring to those who have come, have been
poorly attended and have certainly not received the kind of
publicity that Maple Leaf Sports & Entertainment—which
owns the Toronto Maple Leafs hockey team, the Toronto
Raptors basketball team, Maple Leaf Gardens, and other concerns—can generate.

The same seats that are filled for hockey games and concerts
are largely empty for the forums. Each year the Drydens and
their collaborators review their efforts and continue to ask:
"What is it that we can do that will make the biggest difference?" Several of the survivors believe that public service
announcements by high profile players such as Mats Sundin or
Curtis Joseph, televised during a hockey game, could catapult
child abuse into the public consciousness. Because the survivors were abused in a hockey environment and they know
how important the game is to Canadians, they continue to see
hockey-related initiatives as key to addressing child abuse. As
much as the survivors appreciate the efforts of the Drydens,
they are still looking for highly visible and tangible evidence
that the Toronto Maple Leafs are committed to helping children
avoid abuse. It is also possible that whatever the Maple Leafs
undertake, it will never feel like enough to these men because
it can never undo what happened to them.

When the staff of CASAT heard the news of Kruze's suicide,

everyone stopped working and cried together in the middle of the office. By the next day, however, they had decided to take action and speak out—just as Martin Kruze had done so many months before. They invited the staff of the Metropolitan Toronto Special Committee on Child Abuse (now the Toronto Child Abuse Centre) and Art Lockhart of the developing Gatehouse to join them in issuing a press release expressing their sorrow and praising Kruze's work for their common cause. They also announced that they would hold a memorial service at the still-boarded-up Gatehouse on Saturday, November 1. The Gatehouse had been close to Martin's heart, and now it would begin serving its purpose of providing safety and support, whether the building was physically ready or not. Perhaps its dilapidated condition would emphasize the terrible state of support for survivors and increase awareness about abuse in general. The CASAT team and colleagues gathered up all the purple ribbons—the symbol for child abuse awareness—left over from another mediocre October of "raising awareness to prevent child abuse."

The CASAT staff was also worried about the other men who had been abused by Stuckless, but nobody knew who they were or how to reach out to them. They appealed to the media to broadcast their invitation.

They were right to be worried. The men were devastated by Kruze's death. Not only had they lost their vocal leader, they had lost one of themselves. Kruze's ability to appear in command of himself, to participate in interviews, and to offer hope and support to other survivors led many to believe that he had made it to safety. And yet, perhaps better than anyone, the survivors always saw the pain on his face and in his eyes. He was the same as them. He might have been the public face of sexual abuse for a while, but he was still the same person who had lived with its effects, largely on his own, for much of his life. Kruze's fellow survivors knew all about this too.

Martin Kruze's decision to take his own life was less shocking to the men than was Kruze's decision to go public about his sexual abuse. Many had pledged to themselves that they would never reveal what had happened to them, but most had considered or attempted suicide at one time or another. Suicide was conceivable, perhaps even preferable to the pain they were enduring—telling was not.

Some wondered how many others had already ended their lives. Many of the men thought back to others they had known who had killed themselves and who, in retrospect, might have been sexually abused by one of their own abusers. Kruze was likely not the first to commit suicide, but he was sure to be the most remembered.

Sexual abuse seems to be inextricably linked to suicide. The first time Martin Kruze ever told his family about his sexual abuse was when he felt so overcome by it at age twenty-four that he tried to kill himself. As Gary Kruze came to more fully understand the experiences of his brother and the other Gardens survivors, he began to describe sexual abuse itself as "life threatening."

Many people assume that Justice Watt's sentence was the cause of Kruze's death. "We often talk about a triggering event," says Karen Letofsky, co-executive director of the Survivor Support Program in Toronto. "But court cases go bad often and people don't kill themselves. Suicide is so much more complex." Everyone was devastated by the sentence given to Stuckless and then all over again when Martin killed himself four days later. As far as is known, no other survivors have taken their lives, but other men have since attempted to kill themselves.

Letofsky is adamant that the "whole package" must be considered to understand the links between sexual abuse and suicide: the person's history, present circumstances, and feelings of hopefulness or hopelessness about the future. It is dangerous to try to suggest that sexual abuse by itself leads to suicide. For one thing, people who have been sexually abused may come to believe that suicide is a natural outcome of abuse. Although survivors of sexual abuse are acknowledged to be overrepresented among people who commit suicide, there are many abuse survivors who don't kill themselves and who in spite of many hardships and challenges would never think of ending their lives. Michael Coulis is one of those survivors. He was abused as a child when a teenager carried him off from his backyard and molested him. As much as Michael has lived with the effects of his abuse, he has never wanted to kill himself. His wife, however, had been sexually abused and attempted suicide several times. Their troubled marriage and her sudden death as a result of a car accident left Coulis trying to understand why people who have already been victimized then turn against themselves. Although he never met Kruze, Coulis identified strongly with him and with the hurt on his face. Coulis is just one of the many people whom Kruze inspired to break through his cover of secrecy and anonymity.

Some of the survivors questioned the worth of their lives when Stuckless was given such a light sentence. Certainly they questioned their decisions to come forward and the mess many were now living with as their lives and relationships with their families unravelled. They also had firm—but differing—ideas about why Martin Kruze had killed himself, even though they had never talked directly with him about his previous attempts. Each survivor interviewed for this book had a singular explanation: the light sentence was responsible; the effects of sexual abuse are so life-damaging that suicide is inevitable; his family neglected him as a child and later again as an adult; the health system is uncaring and turned him away when he needed it most.

For a long time Martin Kruze lived courageously with his abuse. Many have described him as "larger than life," and he was. He tracked down Gordon Stuckless when the police couldn't find him. He held a press conference in his home and shared details of his abuse that few would dare to reveal. He turned himself into a professional survivor of sexual abuse and went on a mission to raise awareness and help children and adults alike. He even considered himself an instrument of God. He sent Steve Stavro a letter asking for money to fund the reprinting of a handbook on sexual abuse when Maple Leaf Gardens had already made a secret deal with him to keep quiet about exactly that subject. And then he pitched himself off a bridge in broad daylight instead of taking a more private route to ending his life. Few others would have dared or even wanted to have any part of his life. These are just some of the things that set him apart from others.

Every day Martin Kruze lived all the tensions that so many survivors experience day after day: the tension between going public and keeping private, speaking up and keeping silent, connecting with others and feeling alone, hoping and despairing, feeling good and feeling shame. And throughout all of this, he was still Martin Kruze, the boy and later the man who loved taking shots, pushing limits, tapping on tables, charming customers, grabbing attention, and being funny, and who genuinely believed that all creatures—animals and people alike—deserve to be treated with kindness.

But he was still in trouble. He still hurt. He still lived every day in pain. What masqueraded as heroism in the eyes of others may have been the drastic steps he took to rid himself of the awful feelings that he continued to experience. Divulging all the terrible secrets he held inside still wasn't enough. So here was Martin Kruze, public figure, self-declared survivor, hero to countless survivors all very much in search of a hero, and still the private Martin Kruze struggled. A mere eight months after Kruze's startling entry into public life, CBC journalist Rex Murphy would observe that "Martin Kruze's exit is being read by some as the most powerful statement he ever made." If Murphy's assertion is true, it's a tragedy that it took a man's death to make that kind of statement.

It was raining gently Saturday morning, the morning of the memorial service at the Gatehouse. Reporters and camera crews were on hand to record the event. Some visitors hung back by the trees—Art Lockhart wept by one of them. Some stayed in their cars, and others, like Steve Sutton, Derrick Brown, and Derrick's mother, cautiously approached the small group that was starting to form directly in front of the boarded-up Gatehouse. Some people wrote messages on the outside walls, messages to Martin and to each other, messages about sexual abuse. Rain dripped down the messages and soon poured on the people who huddled together with their umbrellas saying a few words but not that many because it was hard to talk about what Martin Kruze had meant to everyone there. That night, long after everyone else had moved on, Derek Goodyear made his own visit to the Gatehouse, because he wanted to be there when he could be alone.

On Sunday, the day following the memorial, the Kruze family held a press conference at the same location. Encouraged by the event held there the day before, they decided the Gatehouse was the right place for them to speak as well. The media had now tripled from the day before. Jayne Dunsmore came—she drove up in her van alone. She read the messages on the walls with tears streaming down her face. Ron and Gary Kruze arrived with their wives and their family lawyer, Arnold Bruner.

They spoke to the press about the devastating loss of their brother and delivered a forceful message to Maple Leaf Gardens and the hospitals that had turned their brother away.

Michael Irving—the man building the monument to survivors of abuse—arrived to talk further with Gary and Teresa about an idea they had discussed on the telephone the day before. Teresa and Gary had been wondering if there was any way that Martin's handprint could still go on the monument. Martin had been planning to attend one of the workshops that Irving organized for survivors but had postponed his visit until after the sentencing date. Now Irving said that yes, Martin's handprint could, even in death, be added to the others that would make up the garment squares of the monument. Although they thought the process seemed a little morbid, the Kruze brothers agreed to go with Irving to the Rosar-Morrison funeral parlour where Martin lay in rest, to take a plaster cast of his hand. The brothers talked to Martin about the times they'd had together—and with each other about what their kid brother had meant to them. Afterwards, Ron and Gary both said it was one of the most memorable and meaningful things they'd ever done.

On Sunday and Monday hundreds of people came to the funeral home to pay their respects: men and women of the Latvian community, friends and relatives of the Kruze family, friends of Martin and Jayne, and many who had never met Martin but had drawn some inspiration from him. Many of the men arrived in jackets with hockey insignias on them.

The funeral took place on Tuesday morning, November 4.

Although it had rained throughout the previous weekend, the day of the funeral was cool, bright, and sunny. The service was held in St. Andrew's Latvian Lutheran Church, just a few blocks east of Maple Leaf Gardens, the same church in which Martin had been baptized and confirmed. Hundreds of people packed the church for the service. Many had never even met Kruze; they came to pay their respects to the man who had touched them in ways that went beyond ties of friendship and family. Kruze's family stood by his casket and received condolences from family members and friends from the Latvian community but mostly from the men and women who identified so strongly with Kruze because of his sexual abuse.

Derrick Brown, Derek Goodyear, Thomas Allan, and Barry and Darryl Bingham came, as did countless others who will never be identified. They all felt broken and shattered. Martin Kruze had been the catalyst for everything that had happened since he had gone public in February of that year—now he was gone.

Peter Mashin, one of the sons of Ron Kruze's godparents, spoke about how Martin had attended Latvian school on Saturdays, played the drums, and mostly stole centre stage at family events. He was the first to bring to life the parts of Martin Kruze that had been overshadowed by his public role as a survivor of sexual abuse at Maple Leaf Gardens. Jayne Dunsmore spoke about Martin's sweet heart and about how long and hard he had battled to reclaim himself and to stay alive. She urged everyone to keep his dreams alive. Georgia Colton of CASAT wept as she spoke of what his actions had meant to other survivors, saying that "he had the courage to step forward and tell others about his humiliation and degradation."

Christie Blatchford wrote in the *Toronto Sun* the next day that Ken Dryden, who sat in the back row, looked as "sad and ruined as everyone else." Dryden had felt he should be at the funeral as a representative of the Leafs, but he didn't know how the family—or anyone else—would feel about his being there. He had finally located a telephone number for the Kruzes and was surprised when Teresa Kruze, the TSN sports commentator, answered. He had never connected the names. She had assured Dryden that the family would welcome his attendance at the funeral.

Following the service, Ken Dryden headed back down the street to Maple Leaf Gardens. A short while later a group of people arrived, telling security they had come from the church and asking if they could meet with him. Dryden agreed and soon found himself talking with a minister and group of survivors of abuse. They were there to tell him that having just come from Martin's funeral, where the church had been filled with mourning and celebrating Martin's life, they couldn't stomach looking down the street at Maple Leaf Gardens, where everything appeared to be business as usual. Would Dryden consider lowering the Canadian flag that waved atop Maple Leaf Gardens to half-mast to commemorate Kruze's death? Dryden carefully told them that it would feel like an empty gesture because the act didn't hold any meaning for him. They talked for a few more minutes, and as the group filed out of his office, one of them stopped and said, "Well, you may see it as a sort of gesture that doesn't mean something, but it may mean something to somebody else, and that's what counts." Dryden realized that the gesture meant a great deal to the people who had come there making the request, and he did have the flag lowered to half-mast that day. There would be many more requests made of Ken Dryden and Maple Leaf Gardens because the question asked most often—after everyone said that something good had to come out of Martin Kruze's death—was, What was Maple Leaf Gardens going to do to finally acknowledge that Martin Kruze and possibly hundreds of other men had been sexually abused in Canada's greatest hockey shrine?

Later that day, the coffin of Arnold Martin Kruze, age thirty-five, was lowered into the ground at York Cemetery, not far from the neighbourhood where he had lived with his brothers and parents for many years. The air was completely still. Three men stood back watching the family say their good-byes to Martin. When the family got into their cars to return to the church for a small reception, the men approached the grave. There Derrick Brown, Thomas Allan, and Derek Goodyear— who had only seen each other at court and hardly knew one another at all—pledged to their survivor brother Martin Kruze that they would carry out his work and that his life and everything that he had done for them would never be in vain.

IT WAS AN EMOTIONAL DAY

THREE SURVIVORS DESCRIBED how they felt about Kruze's death and about the Gatehouse memorial service.

> I felt like I had to be there that day—it was pouring rain, and there was the board or something that they had there, and people were writing little things on it, and putting flowers on it and all kinds of stuff there. It was a very emotional day for me, thinking of why we were all there, and I guess that's why I wanted to do so much for these guys, because I met somebody who was like me, played hockey—and this fellow really took something that I never knew I had inside of me and that was being able to acknowledge the fact that, "Yeah, there is a problem with you, Derrick, you do have problems." And I thought . . . hey, we could join up and just kind of wreck the world and say, "This isn't how it's supposed to be; this is how it's supposed to be, 'cause we've lived it, we know what it's about." And, it was very heartbreaking that day, being down there. —Derrick Brown
>
> I cried, you know, mainly because I didn't get to know the man. . . . It was a miserable morning, but I felt like I had to be there, to be in his presence.

And knowing at that time I thought it was a type of memorial service for him, where it was going to be all these people and stuff like that, and we show up and it's only a little thing, it's not part of the funeral service. But it was, basically, it was a good experience for me to be down there and be part of that. —Steve Sutton

It just broke my heart. I mean, I know how he felt. When my wife left me and took my kid. I stood at that viaduct, you know. When my girlfriend killed herself, when my best friend OD'd on heroin, when I was stabbed in the joint, when I was shot, when I couldn't keep a job, when I couldn't stop sticking a needle in my arm, day after fucking day, I found myself in front of that thing going, "Why?" And then when that piece of shit got two years, he just couldn't take it. This is what I think, I don't know. I wish that I'd been there, or somebody would have been there to just go, "Get off. Get the fuck down here. What are you doing?" But it's not quite that trivial. I mean, he was never, ever given a chance from day one. I mean, background. None of us were really given a chance. We were just meat for the beast. —James Rainer

MARTIN'S HOPE

If I can help just one person... then all of this will have been worth it.
—Martin Kruze on *Jane Hawtin Live,*
        February 26, 1997

IT HAS BEEN FIVE YEARS since Martin Kruze made his trip to the police station with Jayne to report his abuse, both of them wondering if he would make it through the doors and later wondering if anything would come of it. More than anything, Martin wanted the abusers brought to justice; he wanted Maple Leaf Gardens to take responsibility for allowing the abuse to occur and he wanted therapy for the victims, "paid for by Maple Leaf Gardens."

Martin Kruze set out a tall order, and true to form he got just about everything he wanted. Tragically, he didn't live to see how it all would unfold. It would take his death and many acts of courage and determination by his family and supporters, and most of all by his fellow survivors, to carry it through—but they would do it.

Martin Kruze would have taken great satisfaction in hearing Steve Stavro apologize to the men who were sexually abused at Maple Leaf Gardens and publicly promise to ensure that something like that would never happen again. Maple Leaf Gardens would also pay for counselling, as Martin had always wanted. It would have pleased him to know that it was his father and his brother Gary who pushed for it to happen.

As much as Martin enjoyed the spotlight on him and his cause, he probably would have been uncomfortable with a forum held in his honour. But he would have wanted professionals and survivors and their families to come together and help each other to raise awareness about sexual abuse and get more immediate help for survivors. What would it have meant to Martin to see Derek Goodyear standing on the VIP platform during opening ceremonies at centre ice in Maple Leaf Gardens telling everyone sitting in the golds and reds that he has learned he has nothing to be embarrassed or humiliated about as a survivor of sexual abuse? And to then see everyone rise to their feet and cheer him for his courage?

Martin would have liked the survivor panels. Hearing men and women talk about the big and little things they do each day to help themselves had always helped him. If he had heard Ken Comeau say that one day he'd like to speak on a panel, Martin Kruze might have known Comeau was one person he had helped. Today youth forums are held in the Air Canada Centre, and teens come from schools throughout Toronto to hear what Leafs idols like Curtis Joseph have to say about child abuse. Martin hadn't thought of that one, but he most certainly would have been honoured to know that he had played a role in making it happen. Ken and Lynda Dryden work closely with the Canadian Centre for Child Abuse Awareness, which manages the fund set up in Martin's memory, and the Toronto Child Abuse Centre. The Toronto Maple Leafs and a number of their corporate partners, like Shoppers Drug Mart, donate the proceeds of many initiatives, such as the sale of the annual official Leafs calendar, to these and other related organizations. A life skills scholarship has also been created to support survivors of child abuse.

One can imagine Martin Kruze dancing at the opening of the Gatehouse in June 1998 and then calling often to see what he could do to help. The Gatehouse opened shortly after Martin's brother Ron died of pancreatic cancer, diagnosed only a few months earlier. One can also imagine how good Martin would have felt placing his handprint on a square at the Survivor Monument, right next to the ones that his fellow survivors made. Martin no doubt would have called up all of his media contacts to make sure they covered the arrival of the monument in September 2001—just in time for Child Abuse and Neglect Prevention month. He would have especially enjoyed it because Maple Leaf Gardens was assisting with the funding, and they were going to give it the best home that Martin could ever hope for: right outside the new Air Canada Centre for all the world to see.

Martin probably would have urged the survivors who decided to sue Maple Leaf Gardens to stick with it and not let the lawyers run the show. Looking back on his own experience, he might have figured out that this time around the men should have a lot more control over the process than he did. They should have been able to team up and tell Maple Leaf Gardens and its insurers what they wanted to happen. Instead, he would have seen them scared, alone, and upset. Most likely, Martin would have agreed with the survivors that no matter how much they got, it would never repair what had been done to them. But at least the money might help them get something started or reduce some of their debts. For Martin, the important thing was always that Maple Leaf Gardens should be paying.

In May 1999, after a seven-month trial and ten days of jury deliberations, John Paul Roby was convicted on thirty-five counts of sexual assault, labelled a dangerous offender, and sentenced to an indefinite number of years in prison. Martin Kruze might have wondered why Roby's penalty was so much harsher than that of Gordon Stuckless. Two and a half years later, Roby died in prison of an apparent heart attack.

In August 1998, the Crown had won its appeal and Stuckless's original sentence was extended to five years. But the longer term meant that probation and chemical castration were no longer available in law. What would Martin's reaction have been to that development?

It is easier to imagine what his reaction might have been in February 2001, when the Correctional Service of Canada established that Stuckless "was unlikely to re-offend before the end of his sentence and so declined to recommend that the National Parole Board force him to serve out his entire five-year jail term." He would certainly have agreed with the man he called his "personal detective," Dave Tredrea, when he lamented that if they can't get it right with someone as high-profile as Gordon Stuckless, what are they doing with all of the other offenders who haven't got the press sniffing after them?

Even more amazing and disgusting, according to information from Toronto prosecutors, reported by Christie Blatchford, Stuckless was overheard after his initial sentencing saying that he regretted Kruze had not killed himself sooner. Prosecutors alleged that a guard overheard Stuckless say that it was "too bad that piece of shit didn't do that sooner. Then I wouldn't be here." That information, which Crown attorneys had ready to send to the parole board to support their argument that Stuckless should not be granted early release, was accompanied by a handwritten statement from another jail guard who claimed that he had discovered "pictures that depicted child pornography taped to a magazine in Stuckless's cell," although the guard did write that he was unsure whether the pictures belonged to Stuckless or his cellmate.

The outrage that accompanied the decision to release Stuckless early was comparable to that which surrounded his trial in October 1997. In a press conference the day following the decision, Gary Kruze described his reaction to the news: "I just started to shake. I'm in shock. I'm disgusted and very disappointed. [Stuckless] has ruined so many lives. Why don't the courts and parole boards realize how serious this is? We've got to stop this from happening." Martin Kruze would have been proud of his older brother.

Survivor Derrick Brown—who graced the cover of the February 9, 2001, *National Post,* with Martin's mother in the background—held back tears as he told the media assembled at the conference that "once again, we're being stepped on. As a survivor, I feel once again they don't care." You're right, Kruze would no doubt have agreed, and he might have thanked Brown for taking care of things where he left off. He might also have told Brown how proud he was of him for getting and holding on to his job and for laying off the alcohol—most of the time. He would have understood Steve Sutton when he said that he was afraid of running into Gordon Stuckless on the street someday. He would also have admired Sutton for becoming an active member of Alcoholics Anonymous and remaining clean and sober for five years. And he would have been impressed by Ken Comeau, who, when he heard that Stuckless was being released in spite of all the reasons that he shouldn't have been, stayed calm and focused on himself and his own life, saying that Gordon Stuckless had already taken twenty years of his life and he wasn't going to get another second.

Most of all, Martin Kruze would have seen more and more men and women saying that they were survivors of abuse. We can imagine him wishing them well and wishing that he could have spoken up sooner about his own abuse. We know that he would have asked everybody who has started to speak out publicly—after his disclosure and in the wake of his death—to take care of themselves first. You can't save anybody else if you can't save yourself, he would have said.

If only he could have believed that he was worth saving. Arnie Kruze, Martin Kruze—the boy who loved to play hockey, the aspiring drummer, the snappy dresser, the man with the handsome looks and the devilish smile. We like to think he's smiling at all of the survivors who are quietly making it.

Sources

RESEARCH FOR THIS BOOK BEGAN in the summer of 1998. Much of the material is drawn from Martin Kruze's private notes and correspondence and from copies of his clinical records, which he secured from many hospitals and mental health services. We also drew on the extensive media coverage and court documents. We conducted interviews from the summer of 1998 to the fall of 2001 with many people: some of Martin's family, friends, and partners; men who were abused by George Hannah, John Paul Roby, and Gordon Stuckless both inside and outside of Maple Leaf Gardens; the officer who was the lead investigator for the cases; other men and women who were victimized under separate circumstances altogether; experts in the areas of sexual abuse, trauma, and suicide who provided general comments about the issues but not information pertaining to specific clients; and individuals who became instrumental in helping Maple Leaf Gardens, Limited, formulate its response to Martin's death. Others, such as Jim Dickinson (Martin's therapist for five years) and Susan Orlando and Jim Hughes (Crown attorneys who prosecuted Roby and Stuckless) declined to be interviewed in order to protect client confidentiality or because of ongoing legal and civil cases.

The individuals who were interviewed, in alphabetical order, are: Iland Akbar, Thomas Allan, Barry Bingham, Darryl Bingham, Marque Brill, Derrick Brown, Georgia Colton, Ken Comeau, Michael Coulis, Manny DeSousa, Ken Dryden, Lynda Dryden, James Dubro, Jayne Dunsmore, Dawn Forrest, Sylvia Fraser, Derek Goodyear, Jim Hall, Rob Hawkings, Jane Hawtin, Steven Haylestrom, Hayden Jason Jones, Michael Irving, Vicki Kelman, Sheldon Kennedy, Kemmy King, Gordon Kirke, Gary Kruze, Imants Kruze, Teresa Kruze, Sanderson Layng, Karen Letofsky, Arthur Lockhart, William Marshall, Ronald Masters, Christopher Miller, James Rainer, Diana Roman, Rudy Ruttiman, Brian Silber, Kim Snow, Steve Sutton, Dave Tredrea, Jackie Turner, and Clifford Wright.

For each section of the book, we list the individuals interviewed (in alphabetical order) as well as the sources of quotations (in order of appearance). The interview dates provided are the month and year in which the interviews began; many interviews extended for several months beyond the month noted.

PROLOGUE

Epigraph: Letter written by Martin Kruze to the Metropolitan Toronto Police (January 24, 1997).

Interviews: Jayne Dunsmore (January 2001); Detective Dave Tredrea (January 2001).

CHAPTER ONE

Epigraph: "The Life Story of Arnold Kruze (Bayview Junior High, 1974)," from Kruze's personal materials.

Interviews: Gary Kruze (September 1999); Imants Kruze (February 2001).

Additional: Letter from Astrida Kruze to Imants Kruze (November 1984). Hospital and clinical reports from 1984 to 1994 documenting Martin Kruze's personal history, and his handwritten notes submitted to Ontario's Criminal Injuries Compensation Board (January 1994).

This Can't Be Happening
Interview with Clifford Wright (June 1999).

CHAPTER TWO

Epigraph: Handwritten notes by Martin Kruze (1994).
Interviews: Manny DeSousa (August 2001); Gary Kruze (September 1999); Imants Kruze (February 2001).
Additional: Martin Kruze's handwritten and typed notes prepared for his civil suit against Maple Leaf Gardens, Limited (dated June 1992 to January 1994). Letter from Martin Kruze to the Metropolitan Toronto Police (January 24, 1997). Quotation from Charles Wilkins, "Maple Leaf Gardens (and how it got that way)," in *Maple Leaf Gardens: Memories and Dreams, 1931 to 1999* (Toronto: Maple Leaf Sports and Entertainment Limited, 1999), pp. 53-54. Quotation from Rosie DiManno, "Crowds: Packing them in," in *Maple Leaf Gardens: Memories and Dreams, 1931 to 1999* (Toronto: Maple Leaf Sports and Entertainment Limited, 1999), p. 84.

I'm Still Trying to Find Out What the Hell Was Going On
Interview with Brian Silber (June 1999).

CHAPTER THREE

Epigraph: Interview with Diana Roman (February 2001).
Interviews: Gary Kruze (September 1999); Diana Roman (February 2001).
Additional: Manuscript article by James Dubro for *Saturday Night* magazine (Summer 1997). Letter from Gary Kruze to Arnie Kruze (December 6, 1990). Martin Kruze's typed and handwritten notes prepared for his civil suit against Maple Leaf Gardens,

Limited (dated June 1992 to January 1994). Hospital and clinical reports about Martin Kruze from 1984 to 1994.

My Father Would Have Killed Him
Interview with Iland Akbar (August 1999).

CHAPTER FOUR
Epigraph: Martin Kruze's handwritten notes (1994).
Interviews: Gary Kruze (September 1999).
Additional: Report written by Jim Dickinson for Ontario's Criminal Injuries Compensation Board (January 10, 1995). Judgement by David English and Linda Abrams of the Criminal Injuries Compensation Board (February 2, 1995). Letter from Martin Kruze to the Metropolitan Toronto Police (January 24, 1997). Martin Kruze's typed and handwritten notes prepared for his civil suit against Maple Leaf Gardens, Limited (dated June 1992 to January 1994). Out-of-court agreement ("Full and Final Release") reached between Maple Leaf Gardens, Limited, and Martin Kruze (November 17, 1995). Letter from Susan Vella to Cliff Fletcher, president of Maple Leaf Gardens, Limited, regarding pending action (January 19, 1993). Suit filed by Susan Vella on behalf of Martin Kruze against Maple Leaf Gardens, Limited, on December 23, 1993, docket number 93 QC 46434 (Ontario Court of Justice, General Division). Correspondence between Susan Vella and Martin Kruze (June 1992 to March 1997). Correspondence between Susan Vella and Borden & Elliot (February 1994 to December 1995).

I Felt Hopeless
Interview with Darryl Bingham (November 1998).

CHAPTER FIVE
Epigraph: Press release written by Martin Kruze (February 18, 1997).
Interviews: Jayne Dunsmore (February 1999); Gary Kruze (September 1999).
Additional: Letter (unsent) from Arnold Martin Kruze to Imants Kruze (February 4, 1997). Letter from Martin Kruze to Teresa

Kruze (February 10, 1997). Martin Kruze's notes and correspondence to Dale Brazao at the *Toronto Star*. Statement to
the media by Brian Bellmore on behalf of Steve Stavro
(February 24, 1997). Out-of-court agreement ("Full and
Final Release") reached between Maple Leaf Gardens,
Limited, and Martin Kruze (November 17, 1995). Corres-
pondence between Susan Vella and Martin Kruze (June
1992 to March 1997). Personal communications between
Martin Kruze and Cathy Vine (April 1997 to October
1997). Press reports: Rosie DiManno, "Innocent gesture
cause for concern at crazy Gardens," in the *Toronto Star*
(February 26, 1997), p. A7; Dave Perkins, "Leaf brass have
heads firmly stuck in the sand," in the Toronto Star
(February 25, 1997), p. C1; Steve Simmons, "The Last
Word," in the *Toronto Sun* (February 25, 1997), p. S16;
Michael Valpy, "Misbegotten values times three," in the
Globe and Mail (February 25, 1997), p. A15.

Nobody Knew about It
Interview with Ken Comeau (June 1999).

CHAPTER SIX
Epigraph: Interview with Detective Dave Tredrea (January 2001).
Interviews: Thomas Allan (April 2000); Barry Bingham (November
1998); Derrick Brown (May 1999); Ken Comeau (June 1999);
Derek Goodyear (October 1998); Brian Silber (June 1999);
Steve Sutton (March 1999); Detective Dave Tredrea (January
2001); Clifford Wright (June 1999).
Additional: Quotation from Paul Quarrington, "Introduction," in *Maple
Leaf Gardens: Memories and Dreams, 1931 to 1999* (Toronto:
Maple Leaf Sports and Entertainment Limited, 1999),
p. 32. Press reports: Rosie DiManno, "Gardens brass show
how not to handle a crisis," in the *Toronto Star* (February
25, 1997), p. A6; Michael Grange, "Gardens stops short of
apology," in the *Globe and Mail* (February 25, 1997), pp. A1,
A8; Lois Kalchman, "Hockey family shocked by sex abuse
of son, 13," in the *Toronto Star* (June 11, 1988), p. B3; Lois
Kalchman, "Gardens warned of sexual predator in '88," in

the *Toronto Star* (February 23, 1997), pp. A1, A16; Philip Mascoll and Dale Brazao, "Gardens on abuse: It's not our duty," in the *Toronto Star* (February 25, 1997), p. A1.

The Pain Doesn't Go Away
Interviews with Thomas Allan (April 2000); Ken Comeau (June 1999); Brian Silber (June 1999); Clifford Wright (June 1999).

CHAPTER SEVEN

Epigraph: Interview with Sylvia Fraser (August 1999).

Interviews: Sylvia Fraser (August 1999); Jane Hawtin (June 1999); Michael Irving (December 1998); Gordon Kirke (March 1999); Art Lockhart (November 1998).

Additional: Martin Kruze's media appearances: *Canada* AM (February 24, 1997); *The Dini Petty Show* (March 1997); *Jane Hawtin Live* (March 6, 1997); *Oprah* (May 8, 1997). Martin Kruze's handwritten notes and personal materials (1997). Personal communications between Martin Kruze and Georgia Colton (April to October 1997) and between Kruze and Cathy Vine (April to October 1997). Letter from Martin Kruze to Steve Stavro (August 19, 1997). Press reports: Rex Murphy, on CBC *Newsmagazine* (January 5, 1998).

I Would Draw a Picture of a Shattered Mirror
Interview with Marque Brill (December 1998).

CHAPTER EIGHT

Epigraph: Reported by Donn Downey, "Gardens pedophile given two-year term," in the *Globe and Mail* (October 28, 1997), p. A1.

Interviews: Derek Goodyear (October 1998); Art Lockhart (November 1998); William Marshall (July 1999); Detective Dave Tredrea (January 2001).

Additional: Press reports: Rosie DiManno, "No justice in sentence for Stuckless" in the *Toronto Star* (October 29, 1997) p. C1; Donn Downey, "Gardens pedophile given two-year term," in the *Globe and Mail* (October 28, 1997), p. A1; Gary Oakes, "Sex abuser jailed less than 2 years," in the *Toronto*

Star (October 28, 1997), p. A1. Appeal of the judgement by Justice David Watt sentencing Gordon Stuckless in *Regina v. Stuckless* (August 10, 1998), 41 O.R. (3d) 103 (Court of Appeal for Ontario), Abella, Austin, and Borins JJ.A.

The Sentence Was a Slap in the Face
Interviews with Barry Bingham (November 1998); Ken Comeau (June 1999); Derek Goodyear (October 1998); Brian Silber (June 1999); Steve Sutton (March 1999).

CHAPTER NINE
Epigraph: Martin Kruze quoted by Christie Blatchford in "Kruze reached out in death," in the *Toronto Sun* (October 31, 1997), p. 5.
Interviews: Jayne Dunsmore (January 2001); Gary Kruze (September 1999); Imants Kruze (February 2001).
Additional: Press reports: Christie Blatchford, "Kruze reached out in death," in the *Toronto Sun* (October 31, 1997), p. 5. Michael Ondaatje, *In the Skin of a Lion* (Toronto: Vintage Canada, 1987), p. 27.

You Have This Intense Feeling of Abandonment
Interviews with Ken Comeau (June 1999); Derek Goodyear (October 1998); Steven Hiller (December 1998).

CHAPTER TEN
Epigraph: Interview with Gordon Kirke (March 1999).
Interviews: Thomas Allan (April 2000); Barry Bingham (November 1998); Derrick Brown (May 1999); Georgia Colton (April 1997); Michael Coulis (November 1998); Jayne Dunsmore (January 2001); Ken Dryden (December 1998); Derek Goodyear (October 1998); Jane Hawtin (June 1999); Michael Irving (December 1998); Gary Kruze (September 1999); Teresa Kruze (October 2001); Karen Letofsky (June 1999); James Rainer (February 1999); Steve Sutton (March 1999); Detective Dave Tredrea (January 2001).
Additional: Press reports: Christie Blatchford, "Martin Kruze was more than a victim," in the *Toronto Sun* (November 5, 1997), p. 5; Rex Murphy, CBC *Newsmagazine* (January 5, 1998).

It Was an Emotional Day
Interviews with Derrick Brown (May 1999); James Rainer (February 1999); Steve Sutton (March 1999).

EPILOGUE

Epigraph: Martin Kruze on *Jane Hawtin Live* (February 26, 1997).

Interviews: Thomas Allan (April 2000); Ken Comeau (June 1999); Manny DeSousa (August 2001); Derek Goodyear (October 1998); Steve Sutton (March 1999); Detective Dave Tredrea (January 2001).

Additional: Press reports: Christie Blatchford, "You do the crime, you do some of the time," in the *National Post* (February 9, 2001), p. A14; Canadian Press, "Maple Leaf Gardens pedophile Roby dies," in the *Toronto Star* (November 8, 2001), p. A1; press conference with Gary Kruze; Peter Kuitenbrouwer, "Officials say decision to free pedophile was made carefully," in the *National Post* (February 9, 2001), pp. A1, A8; Steve Stavro's apology published as a press release (January 23, 1998).

INDEX

3 3132 01941 6363
OKANAGAN REGIONAL LIBRARY